I LVE Mondays

A guide to finding joy in your work

JESS STUART

ISBN 978 0 9951425 0 3   (softcover)

ISBN 978 0 9951425 1 0   (kindle)

Other books by Jess Stuart:

A Rough Guide to a Smooth Life (2015)   9781504343817

Like a Girl (2018)   97781973983460

The Superwoman Survival Guide (2020)   9780473517908

*This book is dedicated to all those who've made the leap
to do something they love*

And to those who are about to

Contents

Introduction

ACCORDING TO THE 2018 Great Place to Work report, only 40% of us are happy at work. That means a massive 60% of us are unhappy.

Is it possible to do work we love and get paid for it? Why do so many of us dislike our jobs, and what's the impact on our health and happiness? Society models a version of career success that revolves around status, titles and salary, not passion, purpose and happiness.

What would it be like to jump out of bed each Monday excited about the week ahead? To feel purpose and accomplishment at the end of each day and make a difference whilst paying the bills?

This book uncovers the secret to finding work you love and if that's not your current job, how to find a new one. Master the art of work–life balance and get the job you've dreamed of. Discover the joy of finding meaning and purpose in the work that you do, working for a company that aligns with your values, with people you trust, where you get to use your skills and learn.

I spoke to many people who do just that, from those who left law and banking to start their own business to those learning, growing and contributing in their nine-to-five employment, including healthcare professionals, government workers, project managers, tech developers and more. Despite the diversity of those I spoke to, there were recurring themes that made people love their work. These were echoed by the experts I've quoted throughout the book and their own experience and observations.

These case studies are written in the interviewee's own words and can be found throughout the book, interspersed between chapters. In some instances the names have been changed or surnames omitted to protect the anonymity of individuals or organisations.

These interviews have enhanced the project beyond my expectations. It was such a pleasure to hear how and why these people enjoyed their work and about their journey to this point. I hope it inspires you too.

So many of us are unhappy at work, even though we spend at least one third of our days there whilst living for the weekend. I believe this is linked to our mental health epidemic and our unhappiness levels across the world today.

I know it doesn't have to be like this. I've been there, and I've navigated that journey to find a job I love. This book will help you do the same.

First, it's important to understand what it is about your job that's making you dissatisfied, so you can decide on your next step.

In the first few chapters we'll look at markers of employee engagement and the three main elements that contribute to job satisfaction: what you do, how you do it and who you do it with, including how to find purpose in your work and find a job that aligns with your values and strengths.

We'll explore new ways of working beyond the traditional nine-to-five model and the impact leadership has on our job satisfaction, including what to do if you don't get on with your boss!

By this point, you'll have a better idea of how to improve your work situation and whether you need to stay or leave your current role. But it's not always easy to take action, so we'll look at why we choose the jobs we do and what makes them so hard to leave, including overcoming our fears and taking that next step.

If you've decided by this point that it's time to look for a new job, the chapters towards the end of this book will help find your dream position: developing your brand, networking, preparing a CV, acing a job interview and negotiating your salary.

The final chapter helps us understand the habits for high

performance, sustaining our energy, staying well and the importance of mindset. That means learning the difference between busyness and productivity, managing workloads, prioritising self-care and beating perfectionism.

Experience what it feels like to jump out of bed every Monday morning knowing you make a difference, and sustain high performance to continue to grow in a career you love.

If this is your current job, learn how to negotiate better pay, career development and progression as well as master the art of work–life balance to perform at your peak. Or maybe it's not your current job and you need to make a change – well, let this book show you how to find a new one and prepare to make that transition.

Monday blues

I'm on the bus at 8am, it's raining, it's Monday morning. I look around; darkened faces bury themselves deep in their devices, seeking an escape from the week ahead. Beneath the wet coats, eyes are sunken, mouths downturned – people look glum. I face the window and watch more of the same trudge past as we stop at the lights. A slow, zombie-like procession seems to be emanating from the train station as suits and umbrellas struggle towards their high-rises – not a smile in sight.

I fidget in my too-tight shoes and uncomfortable office attire and think of a million other places I'd rather be. I ask myself the same question I ask every morning on the bus into work. Why are we doing this? Does it have to be this way?

For many years the answers that came back were always yes; I need the money, it's what everyone else is doing, this is city life. If I want the house, the holidays, the car, then I need this job to pay for it.

They'd come on around 3pm on a Sunday – the blues. I'd start to realise the weekend was nearing a close, even though it felt like it had just started. They tended to last until Friday, but Monday morning was always the hardest part of the week.

Friday morning everyone seems to have more of a spring in their step. We're dressed in jeans for casual Friday, the week is almost behind us, a less busy day ahead and the weekend in sight.

Some of us work from home on Fridays so don't even need to face the commute, and those that do have Friday-night drinks to look forward to. Most of us do a lot more social collaboration on a Friday than work emails and meetings. We all have one eye on the weekend, and as a result there are more smiles on the bus, less dread across the faces that emerge from the station and a spring in the step of those making their way to their office high-rises.

We wait all week until Friday; we live for the weekend. But work is part of life; they are not separate. Life doesn't start when work stops. This is why it's so important we enjoy our jobs. We spend so much time there it's bound to impact everything from our mood to our health and ultimately our happiness. We can't just wait for the weekend to live (and then only enjoy it until the Sunday-night blues kick in) or wait until retirement to live a life we dream of, free from a job we simply don't enjoy.

For years we've been conditioned to think we have to work for someone else and have to earn more money to have a good life, gain more titles and status to be successful and valued. This is at odds with what the research is showing makes us happy – more time, family, love and making a difference in the world.

The bottom line is if we can find something that utilises our skill set, challenges us to learn and grow, aligns to our values and gives us a sense of purpose, we've cracked it. It won't feel like work, but we will get paid for it.

Most of us are so busy on the hamster wheel trying to earn more, climb the ladder, pay off the mortgage or just complete the to-do list. We've not had time to think about how our jobs or careers align to the bigger questions in life or how they might be contributing to our happiness.

Do you know your values? Have you talked about your strengths? Do you know what your ideal job is? You might have a career plan, but does it include those things or just how to earn more and get promoted?

These days, I love what I do and the flexibility it gives me. Wearing what I want to the office because it's my spare room. Starting when I want, going to yoga in the middle of the day and taking an afternoon off when the sun is out. It's not that I don't work hard; I do. In fact, from an hourly rate perspective, some weeks in the early days, I'd be earning less than minimum wage. But the difference is I love what I do, so it doesn't feel like work. I might work until 8pm one day and take the next off. It's the freedom I always wanted, and when I do work hard, it's not as stressful because it doesn't feel like work.

Sometimes, when I'm walking the dog, I'll have an idea and be so excited about it my pace quickens and I'm practically running the dog back home so I can get into my office and start work to get this idea into action. That had never happened to me before!

At the weekends I have a rule with my partner – it's family time, and I stay out of the office, but it's so tempting. If she's outside mowing the grass or goes and meets friends for coffee, I have to admit to sneaking in there – because I want to and I enjoy it. This is a million miles from where I used to be.

How I found a job I loved

I remember a career counsellor at school asking me if I'd 'like to work in an office like my mum' but it was more of a suggestion than a question. I suspect she had a list of girls' jobs and boys' jobs in front of her too.

We're not taught this stuff at school, and society models a version of career success that revolves around status, titles and salary, not passion, purpose and happiness.

If I was going to do a job aligned to my strengths and passions, then I was probably going to become a professional soccer player, but as a girl in rural England, I was about 20 years too early! This wasn't an option.

In fact, nor were many passion jobs. There was a distinct line between work and passion, earning money and having fun, making a living and making a life. I think that's where so many of us got it wrong.

So I worked my way through offices, industries and countries and gained experience and skills as I went, each time gaining promotions and more money. This was the prescribed ladder for career success. I fell into HR by virtue of working in an admin role for training companies, recruitment companies and eventually local government, who funded my HR qualifications by way of evening classes.

There were bits of it I enjoyed, I guess, when I look back, but I found myself drifting to new jobs every two years or so because I got bored. The prospect of a change always filled me with the hope 'this time it'll be different'.

My dream job was always just around the corner, but the trouble was I was following the same recipe and expecting it to make me happier than it had done before.

Each time I resigned I'd think, I'm going to try something new this time, I don't think this is for me. But what else could I do? This was all I knew, this was what I'd trained for, and it was a 'good' job. So I'd fall back into the same roles, the same unhappiness and lack of fulfilment.

After all, it was my job, it wasn't supposed to make me happy, that was what I did after 5.30pm. Its purpose was to earn me money so I could enjoy life and set up a good pension so I could retire at some very distant point in the future. It did earn me money, and it seemed to be the recipe everyone else was following, so who was I to question if we'd got it wrong?

When I progressed through school there were distinct possibilities as a girl. Nursing and teaching were popular. Anything manual was not, so doing something practical like building or being an electrician or a mechanic was out of the question. Business skills were something else not really necessary for girls. After all, how many of us were really going to be left in charge of a whole business or start up our own? That was a ridiculous notion back then. Well, here we are!

I do remember doing a career survey at a careers day once. It was on a computer the size of my house, back in the days before we knew about algorithms, and I'm not sure what I did, but the answer was not what anyone was expecting. I answered the questions as Mum stood behind me, hoping it would spit out lawyer, doctor or similar. The lady in charge of this giant computer tentatively passed us the printout. Top choice, number one career option, based on my answers ... fence erector.

Now, I'm not sure what algorithm was being used, but knowing my lack of passion for DIY and the lack of skills I have around anything in the garden, I'd say this was not terribly accurate. What courses would I take at A levels for this, and how would I get myself a job? Mum looked a little disappointed. I was mostly confused. I never went on to erect fences.

So how did I eventually join the dots and find a job I loved which also paid my bills? It was a long journey, and it started with the end. The end of my HR career and days in the corporate world.

After establishing my career in New Zealand, there'd been a restructure, and I was offered redundancy or a redeployment promotion which meant moving towns. At the time I was unhappy, but I thought maybe a change of job and scenery would fix that.

Especially the price tag it came with and the company car and benefits. It was the biggest job I'd ever had. The family celebrated like I'd won lotto, and we began planning all the things we'd do with this wealth.

I took the promotion, and a year later, still unhappy in my work, was when I burned out. The impact on my health forced me to choose, and it was at that point I realised there was more to work than money and more money was not always better. So I quit, but this time, instead of saying, 'I think I want to do something different,' for the tenth time and then going straight back into what I knew, I was determined something had to change.

So, at 30, I gave it all up and started again. I wanted to rebuild a life around my passions and to find out if plan A wasn't the answer, as everyone had led me to believe, what was plan B? I gave up my career in the corporate world and decided on a change of direction to follow my passions.

I had always been sold on the reliability of a good job and a regular income. It's scary not to have a pay cheque coming into the bank account every month, and for me it was the first time I wasn't earning since I was 13 and started washing dishes at the local pub.

We often praise people for having a job, getting a job or progressing in their career. We don't often praise them for quitting, especially if they're not sure what they're going to do next.

It's a brave step to take, and often we're not encouraged to be this brave. I remember a friend at the time telling me, as I walked away from my corporate career with the biggest organisation in the country, 'You'll never get another job like that, you know.'

Well, that was the point. I didn't want another job like that. I decided to give myself 12 months to experiment and learn more along the way. I wanted to experience these things and see what worked, and, most importantly, I wanted to find my purpose and a reason to get out of bed in the morning.

I set out on a journey to spend time doing the things I loved, and what it taught me in the process was a lot about myself, my values and how to find purpose and do work we love.

I spent the year writing my first book and doing other things that made my heart sing, including travelling the circumference of Australia in a campervan and visiting Bhutan, the country that operates gross national happiness (GNH) in place of gross domestic product (GDP). I taught English to Buddhist monks in Thailand, lived in yoga ashrams and mindfulness centres, started studying Buddhism and qualified as a life coach and a yoga teacher.

Returning to New Zealand as a qualified coach, yoga teacher and mindfulness practitioner, with no money in my bank account, I began the next chapter of my life. Based in Wellington, where I didn't know anyone.

I began putting on events, coaching and writing more books. It became a way of sharing my learning and helping others grow. From this, I was asked to speak about the books and do trainings and workshops based on the content. I'd found my niche, I'd found my business, and things grew from there.

I never did teach yoga, despite my qualification, but this was all part of the path, experimenting with the things I loved to see what could form a new career.

I've run my own training and coaching business for six years now and written four books. I love combining my HR experience and passion for helping people be their best whilst working in a way that works for me. Where I get to pick my hours and what I focus on and with a sense of purpose that allows me to spring out of bed each morning (well, most mornings!).

There's been so much I didn't know and so much I've had to learn. It hasn't always been easy, but then no job is. Would I swap it or go back? Never in a million years. Not even on the days I had no income for the whole month, no clients and no idea what I was doing.

People thought I was crazy leaving a 'good' job and certainly didn't think going from company car and corporate office to cleaning composting toilets in an ashram was a smart career move, but it turns out it put me on the path to the best job I've ever had.

Now, I'm not suggesting the only way to do a job we love is to get rid of the boss. Running my own business has been hard. The need to learn so much, the mistakes I made along the way and the accountability required.

As anyone running their own business knows, you have to be the accounts department, the marketing department and IT if the laptop goes wrong. Even figuring out the world of publishing was fraught with failure as I improve and learn with each book. I'd equally be happy to do what I do now for someone else and sometimes contract back to local businesses for specific pieces of work.

There's a lot to be said for having a regular pay cheque each month, paid leave and sick pay entitlements. It's also nice to be able to turn up and do a job but let everyone else worry about where the work is coming from, business development and market pivots! Not all of us are cut out to work for ourselves, to motivate ourselves each day even when it comes to doing the stuff we don't like. Some find it hard working alone, without the buzz of an office or the collaboration of the team that surrounds us.

It hasn't always been easy, but I wouldn't change it for the world. My dad still doesn't think I have a job – a real one. I don't go to a place of work and clock in, nor do I earn a salary from an employer. He'll often remark that I'm staying at home whilst my wife goes out to work.

I'm not sure what he thinks I do or where he thinks the books come from, but in his mind the traditional world of work applies, and if its outside of that, it's harder to see as 'work'. A 'proper job' is one that pays a salary, happens at a company and isn't something you particularly enjoy. You certainly don't do it from home in your PJs, drinking cups of tea!

Now, we don't all have to start our own business to experience purpose and make a difference. Nor do we have to quit the corporate world and start a blog or escape to an ashram. This was just my process because it aligned with who I was; yours will be different.

That's what this book is about. It's not suggesting a way forward for you or a blueprint of career success, because we're all different. It's helping you figure out what the best way forward is for you. What kind of person you are, your strengths and values. What you enjoy about your job and why you might want to leave. How to find a job you love and prepare for that move, whether it's in the same industry or organisation you are in now or something totally different – we are all different, and that's what makes us so interesting.

Chapter 1

What's wrong with my job?

Before we look at how we improve our happiness at work we need to understand the factors that help us enjoy our work, and understand why we might be unhappy. What's wrong with my job?

Global co-working organisation Mindspace did a study on employee happiness in December 2019. They surveyed 5,000 people around the world and asked them how they felt about work – what they looked forward to at the office every day, what mattered most to them at their jobs, and what their employers did for them.

They found seven major factors that make people happy: having a sense of purpose, feeling valued, the availability of wellness programs, feeling engaged, working in a collaborative environment, having flexibility, and being in a positive workplace culture.

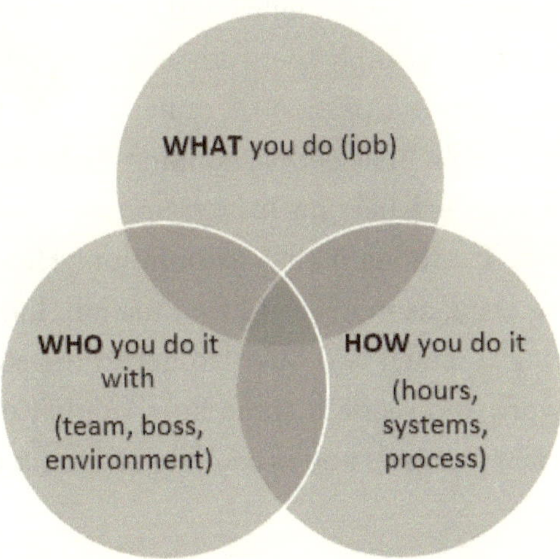

I've boiled this down to three main categories. Our enjoyment at work is made up of what we do, who we do it with and the environment that surrounds us (how we do it), including the systems, process, hours etc.

The job itself might be the problem: it doesn't align to our skills, we've outgrown it and we're bored, or it's too hard and we're stressed.

Then again, it might not be. It could be the toxic people or terrible work culture. Even a good job is a struggle at the wrong company – are the people or the values of the company out of kilter with your own? Maybe your boss is a bully, or you're an introvert working in a team of extroverts.

The relationships we have at work are important, because we spend a lot of time with these people and often rely on them to get our own job done. According to Statistics New Zealand, employees with good relationships with people at work report much higher rates of job satisfaction (91%) than those without (55%).

It could also be the conditions we have to work in or the hours we work. Is it the complicated commute to get to the office that's the problem? How many of us loved our jobs more during Covid-19 lockdown, when we could do them from home in our PJs, without the daily commute, fluorescent lights and broken air conditioning? There's more to it than simply the work we're employed to do.

Yoga has long been a passion of mine, and for many years, I believed it was a hobby that people couldn't make a career out of. Looking at the yoga teachers on Instagram and YouTube and the lululemon chain, I rethought that assumption. However, when I started teaching yoga, as much as I loved the job, I found the early starts and having to catch two buses to get to the studio took the shine off the work and made it something I didn't enjoy. Equally, the hustle for class numbers and marketing of classes drained me. I was much happier living at retreat centres, teaching yoga to guests.

Many teachers and nurses have confessed to me the reasons they went into the career are the bits of their job they love, but they struggle with the system, the red tape, the hierarchy. They want to care for people or help kids learn, but they spend relatively little time actually doing that. It's not the job so much that's the problem, they tell me, but the system it operates in or the environment in which they find themselves. Paperwork, audits, assessments, rosters – the stuff that takes away from the actual job and the bits they love.

How much freedom we have impacts our enjoyment at work too, as do the feeling of belonging and the sense of challenge (no one likes a job that bores them). Equally, being set up for success, having the tools we need to do our job properly and knowing what we're supposed to be doing all come into our job satisfaction.

Most of us have the choice to be in the job we're in; we can leave at any time. But it doesn't always feel that way. Feeling helpless and trapped and lacking autonomy can be massive factors in an unhappy job. Being trusted and having responsibility to deliver our jobs are key.

Employees with high autonomy are more likely to report a good relationship with their manager (72%) and colleagues (76%). This NZ Stats survey went on to say that of the employees with high workplace autonomy, 41% were very satisfied with their job compared to just 27% of employees who reported low levels of autonomy.

What about pay? Sure, this plays a role, but never as big a role as we think. In 2010, Tim Judge and colleagues reviewed 120 years of research and findings from 92 studies. The results indicate the association between salary and job satisfaction is weak. The study shows there is less than 2% overlap between pay and job satisfaction levels. This is consistent with Gallup's engagement research based on 1.4 million employees from 192 organisations across 49 industries and 34 nations, which reports no significant difference in employee engagement by pay level.

In fact, studies show it's often the prospect of receiving a raise that's the motivator, not the actual raise itself. Things that often top salary as a motivator at work include communication, challenge, recognition (non-financial) and autonomy.

Of course, one more reason we might not be happy at work can be closer to home than we think. Sometimes the reason we're unhappy at work is because we're unhappy in life. We bring our troubles to work, or we're in such a funk at home we can't get out of it for the eight hours we're in the office.

You know what it's like when you get out of bed on the wrong side and everything is wrong, everyone is annoying. Imagine this being an everyday experience. It filters through to how we treat colleagues, deal with setbacks at work and cope with the busy days. Sometimes it's not work that's the problem; it's life.

Whilst we're on the subject, what about your outlook? There are certain things that can put us in this funk and impact our work – losing a loved one, a break-up, sickness or personal challenges – but these are all temporary. If it can't be explained by a specific circumstance, there may only be one reason left. If you're a glass-half-empty kind of person regardless of what's happening in life, then often it's not the external things that surround you always at fault.

Sorry to have to bring it up, but it's also necessary to point out. Sometimes the problem is you! We'll cover this more in the chapter on mindset, but if you find your glass is often half empty, that others are always to blame and that you feel like a victim in your job, it might not be the job or your team members that need to change. Sometimes we need to take a long hard look at ourselves, and until we change, nothing else will.

Employee experience – what it means to be engaged at work

Out of the seven factors mentioned, we need to take a closer look at employee engagement. Throughout my HR career, businesses invested time and money into trying to increase the level of employee engagement, meaning those who are happy in their jobs, committed and giving their best, therefore doing their best work. Obviously it was in the companies' best interest, as those giving their best go the extra mile. But it's also in our own best interest as individuals to be happy in our work and engaged in the job we do. Before we look at the factors that we can apply to finding work we love we first need to understand the concept of employee engagement, or, as it's often called, employee experience.

Despite the agendas businesses have to improve their employee engagement, data from millions of surveys continues to tell us that, globally, these statistics are not improving.

To be engaged at work means we're happy, productive and well. It means we enjoy coming to work and do our best work most days. To be disengaged means the opposite, and sometimes it's so bad we become actively disengaged, which means beyond being unhappy in our job and underperforming, we start to sabotage and influence those around us.

Engaged employees don't let problems become an excuse for inaction; they navigate challenges. They seek ways to perform their best and focus on their strengths. They are proactive and take accountability for their performance.

According to Gallup, a staggering 87% of employees worldwide are not engaged. This is based on data from 30 years of surveys and 30 million employees globally. Gallup uses 12 questions as markers of engagement. The more of these questions you can answer yes to, the more likely you are to be engaged in your job.

They tend to fall into four categories connected to our basic needs being met, being valued and supported, and the opportunity to collaborate and then grow.

Basic needs – can I focus and are you enabling me to do my work?
1. Do you know what is expected of you at work?
2. Do you have the materials and equipment to do your work?

Individual needs – know me, value me, help me grow

3. At work, do you have the opportunity to do what you do best every day?

4. In the last seven days, have you received recognition or praise?

5. Does your supervisor, or someone at work, seem to care about you as a person?

6. Is there someone at work who encourages your development?

Teamwork – listen to me, help me see how I contribute

7. At work, do your opinions seem to count?

8. Does the purpose of your company make you feel your job is important?

9. Are your fellow employees committed to doing quality work?

10. Do you have a best friend at work?

Growth – review my contribution and challenge me

11. In the last six months, has someone at work talked to you about your progress?

12. In the last year, have you had opportunities to learn and grow?

In a nutshell, we're more likely to be engaged if we know what's expected of us and have the tools to do our work. It helps if we get to use our strengths and feel valued, supported and listened to but also challenged, so we can grow, be recognised for our efforts and feel safe. It also helps to connect to the bigger picture, to find meaning in the work we do and how it contributes to the wider work of the organisation.

So, let's move on to further break down the what, how and who model and understand the components within each of those categories that will help us identify a job we love. In the next chapter, we'll explore the importance of aligning to our strengths and values to find work that gives us meaning and purpose.

'The opportunity to make a difference to somebody is what gets me out of bed in the morning'

Morena is a hospital theatre services manager and has a nursing background.

It's a unique role and quite new, so I got the chance to come in and create everything from scratch. I do more of the management side of things now, which adds to my real passion as an orthopaedic nurse. Theatre nurses are like the silent angels that do everything whilst you're asleep, so no one ever knows we were there.

As a nurse I would work in theatre, but now I get the chance to set it up, source the equipment, and mentor and support others. I feel like I can make a bigger impact now to make things better for patients and consultants.

I never thought I'd be here now. I had moved home and was contracting for about a year when this job popped up. I knew I had the skills and knowledge for it, and I thought, 'Why not? The worst they can say is no,' so I applied. I really like the team approach. I get to make an impact and build a team culture from scratch.

I had been contracting, and whilst being a contractor is great for control of hours and who you work for, I missed the team approach and you can often feel like the outsider. When I came in there was nothing set up, so it was exciting but scary too. There was no rule book or previous manager to learn from. I ended up doing things I never thought I'd know how to do because of what I was learning. As a nurse we don't have to hire staff or get to think about the kind of equipment improvements we want to bring about to improve the job.

I sometimes miss the hands-on nature and being in the moment with big trauma cases, but I'm content where I am and [with] the impact I have. It's both challenging and rewarding. The opportunity to make a difference to somebody is what gets me out of bed in the morning; the patients are someone's mum or family member.

My advice is don't be afraid to go for it and don't let other people tell you you're not good enough. Don't listen to the stereotypes about what kind of age or appearance you need for certain roles. Even if that doesn't sound like you, don't let it be a reason not to go for something you think you'd love and would be good at. I always tell myself, 'What's the worst they can say?' All they can say is no, so it's worth trying.

Chapter 2

Finding a job you love

I'M DOING A job I love now, but do I love it every day? Is it perfect? No, and I don't believe any job is. Having said that, I wouldn't swap it for the world and wake up every day grateful this is my job. There are things I love about it and then things I don't, and I think this is true of any job.

I get to work for myself, set my hours, choose my clients and do what I love every day, using the skills I have. Yet some days I have to sit and do my accounts or figure out a new algorithm on social media. Some months the numbers don't add up and I wonder how I'm going to pay the bills, and other months I'm thinking of buying a new car. Any job will have its pros and cons; there will always be bits we don't enjoy. However, if we do a job we love, the tough bits become much more palatable.

Is it true that if you do a job you love, you'll never work a day in your life? Well, I've worked harder for myself than I've ever done for anyone else, but I enjoy it, so it doesn't always feel like work. I've made a commitment to my family that I won't go into the office at weekends, but sometimes it's hard; I want to go in there and do a few bits. I look forward to Monday and these days can find it disappointing when there's a public holiday – I used to live for those long weekends in my former life.

Philosopher and civil rights leader Howard Thurman said, "Don't ask what the world needs. Ask what makes you come alive, because the world needs more people who have come alive."

Employment Today magazine quoted a Gallup survey finding a staggering 62% of employees have no passion for their work. What does having passion for your work mean? It's a combination of your values and strengths along with a sense of purpose in what you do.

It's a fundamental part of enjoying what we do – to find purpose in it, to connect to something bigger than ourselves and to see how our efforts are making a difference. This can be in the values of the organisation, helping those we work with or a bigger factor that connects into our reason for being alive. Either way, it gives us a reason to get out of bed in the morning and a feeling of productivity when we know what we're doing makes a difference.

Finding purpose in our work doesn't have to mean working for Amnesty International, saving people from death row, nor does it mean quitting our jobs and starting a yoga blog from Bali.

A friend of mine recently retired, and whilst she doesn't need to work, she took a casual retail assistant job in a fashion store. Her eye for detail and love of fashion means the shop always looks amazing and her creative talents are well employed. She also loves helping other women look and feel great, sharing her knowledge of fashion. This is where her sense of purpose comes from in her job; it's not about the money.

Whether we're a coach writing books to help others, a volunteer teacher aide helping kids learn, a nurse saving lives, a courier delivering flowers to people on their birthday or the guy who puts the widgets in phones, connecting the world, there are so many reasons we find purpose in what we do. The important thing is to connect to your 'why'. Otherwise, it becomes pointless, disheartening and very unfulfilling.

'I use my skills to contribute to something I'm passionate about'
Sophie is a lecturer and former humanitarian worker who has worked

in large-scale emergencies, including war-ridden Darfur, Sudan; post-earthquake Haiti; and Sri Lanka at the end of the civil war.

My heart has always been in this kind of [humanitarian] work and working in teams, yet there was often a hierarchy and collaboration that wasn't as effective as I thought it could be. I've worked with amazing people to build the team as strong as possible, because that's how you operate best in conflict or natural disaster responses. I worked for different NGOs across multiple countries. It's a sector that has its challenges, especially in the leadership space, and I found this a struggle.

Leadership always interested me, and I started teaching at university in between deployments and full time after about 15 years in the aid sector. It's interesting to see what I teach now and see the combination of theory and practice play out in the field. It helped me pick out the gaps and what needed to happen to support people with the development of their leadership and soft skills as well the technical knowledge. It's not just about distributing aid like food but how you distribute it and engage with the teams, communities and stakeholders.

I'd been doing some coaching work on an academic residential leadership skills course with mature students from across the world. At the time I was trying to exit my current job in the US as deputy director emergency response for a large NGO. Working in emergency situations is rewarding, but it's not compatible with a stable and balanced life. The university where I was coaching were looking at starting a new master's programme and informed me of the job opening. I didn't think I would get the job because of high competition and I don't have a PhD. I'm more a pracademic than a pure academic, but this turned into my advantage, as they were looking for someone who can teach theory and practice. I got the job and moved to Melbourne; this was the start of my new career.

I teach the Humanitarian Leadership course in multiple languages across the world, and now I get to use my skills to help contribute to something I'm passionate about but also to improve the industry based on the gaps I've experienced in practice. This course is a transformative experience for students and the community it creates; it's very unique. I love being a part of these people's journeys and the impact this course has on their life and also the humanitarian work they do. Seeing the women grow is something I find particularly rewarding.

It's not always been easy, and in my career I've burned out. I've also been bullied. My line managers have not always supported the work I do or my growth. In one particular example, a manager had opposing values to mine. As the tall poppy, I got ostracised, and by trying so hard to work things out, I burned out.

I took some time off and took care of myself. I challenged the organisation to deal with the issues, and they increased the resources, because we found out I was doing the work of four people. Returning to work gradually and with a change of structure, a new manager and reduced interactions with former colleagues was the best thing.

I was able to take time for me, discover new hobbies and do a couple of courses so returned to work with a much clearer mind. My advice to others in this situation is to take the time you need. Keep positive, although it's not always easy. Keep your values strong and stay true to your integrity.

Purpose: The why behind what we do

Another way of looking at our sense of purpose is something the Japanese call ikigai. It's a concept I wrote about in my first book, *A Rough Guide to a Smooth Life*, when talking about the research around Blue Zones, areas where people live longer than average, and it's directly relevant here too.

The concept of ikigai roughly translates to 'reason for being'. It's a balance of our spiritual and practical needs being met. This balance is found at the intersection where our passions and talents converge with the things the world needs. It is, simply put, our reason for getting out of bed every morning.

It is often portioned into these intersecting categories:

- What you love (your passion)
- What the world needs (your mission)
- What you are good at (your vocation)
- What you can get paid for (your profession)

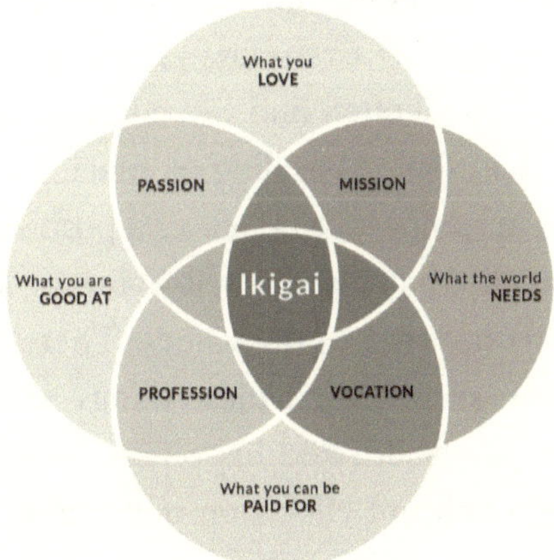

The common mistake we make with this is only looking at what we can get paid for – how do I earn a living? This is how we've approached our day jobs for generations; that has always been their purpose. It's why so many of us end up unhappy in our work, because we only look at this one silo and expect that if we then have money we'll be happy and have more freedom to choose. The fundamental truth of ikigai is that nothing is siloed. Everything is connected.

Finding our passion first then allows us to look at where this is needed and how we might get paid for it.

Don't think you can get paid for your hobbies? Ask photographers, musicians and artists making a living doing exactly that right now.

Ikigai can describe having a sense of purpose in life, as well as being motivated. It entails actions of devoting yourself to pursuits you enjoy and is associated with feelings of accomplishment and fulfilment. The word *ikigai* is also used to describe the inner self of an individual, and a mental state in which the individual feels at ease.

Purpose can be a big thing to consider, and trying to find our purpose can seem overwhelming, especially as a young adult in school or university. It doesn't have to be this big all encompassing pot of gold at the end of a rainbow. If we view our search for purpose in this way we'll often find we're forever searching. Often it's more simple than that. A feeling of making a difference, that what we do helps in some way and leaves a positive impact.

I've experienced what it's like not living in accordance with my purpose, not being true to my values. There have been times when I've not even known what these things were, let alone that they impacted on my health and happiness. The loss of meaning and purpose has significant effects on our health, which makes it so important to our happiness. When our actions match our values and beliefs, we find peace of mind.

We get our sense of self from what we do. Who are you? You may say a mother, a lawyer, an athlete. But you are also more than what you do or your social status. This should not define you or be who you are; it is just what you do.

I once met a guy travelling through New Zealand. He lived in Sydney and worked as an IT professional, but his real passion was photography. His job paid his bills, but he'd use his annual vacation time to come to New Zealand and connect with nature, go walking and take photos. It was during this time he was really alive. We spoke about why he'd only chosen to be alive for four weeks of the year and how he might be able to turn his passion into his job so he could feel alive every day.

We put so much time into doing things that don't matter to us (otherwise known as our day jobs) so maybe one day we can hopefully do something that does matter, when we retire or win lotto, whichever comes first.

It's so important to find purpose in what we do; this is critical if we're to enjoy our work. It might be the connection to an organisation's mission and vision. I might fix drainpipes, but I'm actually helping deliver clean, fresh water to my community. Or perhaps I'm working on a production line in a milk factory, but I'm helping nourish newborn babies across the world.

Think back to when you were a child. What job did you dream of having? It may not be that that's what you should be doing now, but it'll give you some good ideas.

For example, I wanted to be an astronaut. That's not what I should be doing now, but when I unpick what was behind that dream, I find the answers. It was adventurous, out of the ordinary, revered, challenging. I'd be learning new things and at the forefront of making a difference with what I found. These are the things I look for in a job – not necessarily trips into outer space in a rocket wearing a white suit!

Let me ask you about your best day at work – ever. In any job, at any time in your career. What was it? What were you doing that day and with whom? Why was it so good? What skills were you using?

Was it a challenge? What was the outcome or goal of what you were doing? How much fun was it? Why?

Go ahead and do this exercise now. Brainstorm anything that comes to mind when you think about your best day at work and write it down below.

My best day at work

Similarly, your worst day can be just as telling as an exercise. The kind of people we don't want to work with or a lack of vision/ values that align with our own. A job that's so boring the day felt like weeks. Being undermined, micromanaged, not feeling safe. These experiences will tell us about what we need to avoid and also what's important to ensure we do enjoy our next job.

Consider these questions/exercises:

- How do you want to be remembered?
- What are you doing when you're in flow or that makes your heart sing?
- Who do you admire and why?
- Identify your purpose by asking yourself the following questions:

— What's really important to you?

— What do you daydream about?

— When are you having the most fun, what are you doing, who are you with?

— What are your most memorable times/fondest memories?

— How would you live differently if your days were numbered?

— What does your perfect day look like?

— Imagine you'd won the lotto. What would your typical day look like six months later?

'I had to step out and find out who I truly was'
Catherine van der Meulen started out in her family business, SUPRÉ, and the journey since then has led her to found Entrepreneurial Women with Purpose.
It's a combination of my past experiences, the things I love, the things I'm passionate about and the skills I have.
As brand manager of SUPRÉ, I was producing music for

our stores across Australia and New Zealand, developing Healthy Body Healthy Mind education programmes in schools and empowering young women to love the skin they were in. It gave me purpose and used all of my skills, but when we sold the family business, I was looking for a new role that would encompass this.

I realised my whole identity was bundled up in the business too. I had to step out and find out who the hell I truly was. I learned what was important to me and how I want to spend my time and create my future so I could be the owner of that. This had to be work I loved, otherwise why was I taking time away from my children to do it?

Entrepreneurial Women with Purpose has allowed me to take ownership of my time and build a business that encapsulates everything I love. There was no set plan; it evolved. I jumped in and figured it out. I moved to New Zealand alone, with my two children, in search of a slower-paced life and one that has a deeper sense of meaning. I knew it was my time to make a valuable contribution to the world.

I was so busy living on the treadmill of life in Sydney. Getting up at 5am to study before the kids woke up, prepping for the school day, sitting in hours of traffic to get to the office. It's a different pace in rural New Zealand, and that has allowed me more time and space to reflect.

The feedback I get from the women I help makes it all worthwhile. Women who've had opportunities to step forward, have taken the knowledge and support they've gained from our community to start their own business, or amplify their growth. The launch of our Impact Education Programme really fills my cup, supporting women from Vanuatu who are here working temporarily in New Zealand to educate, empower and invest into their world to further activate businesses when they return home. When they come to me with ideas, from community projects to global initiatives, it makes it all worthwhile.

I believe what makes us happy at work are great leaders who are emotionally intelligent and people who allow you to be your whole self and bring your passion to the table. Many of the women I speak to have become disenfranchised with corporate New Zealand; it's why they've left to set up their own business or do something different.

My advice is to be kind to yourself and be committed to your deep sense of purpose so you can say no to what's not aligned and say yes to what will open up other paths for you. Trusting the universe has also helped me. If it's not working, it might just be you're on the wrong path. I had a lot of setbacks in Sydney, going for big roles and continuously getting pushback that the role just wasn't for me, but that's how I ended up here. It wasn't my path; there were reasons I was getting rejected. I moved here, and things began to happen and move in this incredible state of flow. This was my path.

I feared, although I was living a wonderful life in Sydney, that I'd end up living a mediocre life that wasn't underpinned by a depth of purpose. Those intuitive moments when you know something isn't right, you need to evaluate and step forward in a different way. It takes bravery and courage. Not one woman I work with says it's easy and has been smooth, but that's life. We learn from those challenges, and it's part of the journey.

'Ships are safest in the harbour, but it's not what they were built for'

Poppy is a winemaker and owns Poppies in Martinborough with husband Shayne.

I never knew what I wanted to do. The youngest in my family, I grew up on a farm. My siblings had all gone on to be teachers, nurses and physios. I lost a brother and my father at a young age, and this adversity helps bring perspective. It's taught me not to sweat the small stuff and to stay positive. I believe what you radiate out comes back.

I found my passion in wine whilst working as a bungee-jump operator. I loved it, but it was not a long-term career, so I volunteered on my days off at the local vineyard across the road, so I could learn. This felt more like a calling; they encouraged me to train, so I went to university to do my wine degree. I thought I'd be a wine rep initially but was told I was too young at 25; they were giving the jobs to winemakers back then, so that's what I set out to do. I learned a lot from the other vineyards I worked with and am lucky that Shayne and I are a great team with complementary skill sets.

When we built Poppies, people thought we were mad. It was during the global financial crisis, and the wine industry was 95% insolvent. It was our passion, though, and we wanted to do things differently after spending 12 years as a husband-and-wife team at another local vineyard. We decided to create from the heart and make what we love, not what was fashionable; we stayed true to tradition and wanted to put the love back into the industry.

We put in everything we owned and had the support of an amazing group of shareholders who believed in us. I remember those first few months without income; I was sealing the floors and painting the joinery as we finished the building. We've stayed open five days a week, 11–4 every day, since. It's all about consistency and trust, sticking to your values and also the fantastic community that surrounds us and has supported us.

These days, I try to keep looking ahead and not worry what others think. My dad always used to say, 'Ships are safest in the harbour, but it's not what they were built for.'

Aligning to our values

We can find purpose in what we do by aligning our values with our work and that of our workplaces. If I have a value of compassion, it makes sense that I'll need to feel like I'm helping others in the work that I do to be fulfilled. Similarly, if I have a value of achievement, I'm going to want to be challenged, see the fruits of my effort and recognise the results my work is producing.

So what are your values? I remember when I was first asked this question. I didn't even know what values were; I had to google a list and then start picking out words that resonated. Now I have card decks of values I use with individuals and teams to do this similar exercise. It's a powerful way of becoming more self-aware, knowing our values, but it's also a powerful way of connecting teams through shared values.

Here's a list below to get you started. Pick 10 that apply and then narrow that down to your top five. Our values drive the decisions we make and can have a huge bearing on how much joy we find in what we do. They can help us make decisions based on what drives us and therefore in alignment with our values.

My values are all about giving back, freedom and health, so it's no wonder I was unhappy stuck in an office, working for a big corporate in a role that revolved around the bottom line and the money said corporate was making, without the freedom to structure my own day or get out of the fluorescent-lit office. The hours I worked, the travel and back-to-back meetings – it was all at odds with what I valued. I just wasn't aware of it at the time!

Accountability	Equality	Preparedness
Accuracy	Excellence	Professionalism
Achievement	Excitement	Prudence
Adventurousness	Expertise	Reliability
Altruism	Exploration	Resourcefulness
Ambition	Expressiveness	Restraint
Assertiveness	Fairness	Results-oriented
Balance	Faith	Security
Belonging	Fidelity	Self-control
Boldness	Focus	Selflessness
Calmness	Freedom	Sensitivity
Carefulness	Fun	Serenity
Challenge	Generosity	Shrewdness
Cheerfulness	Goodness	Simplicity
Clear-mindedness	Grace	Soundness
Commitment	Growth	Speed
Community	Happiness	Spontaneity
Compassion	Health	Stability
Competitiveness	Helping	Strategic
Consistency	Honesty	Strength
Contentment	Honour	Structure
Continuous	Humility	Success
Improvement	Independence	Support
Contribution	Ingenuity	Teamwork
Cooperation	Inner Harmony	Temperance
Correctness	Inquisitiveness	Thankfulness
Courtesy	Intelligence	Thoroughness
Creativity	Intellectual Status	Thoughtfulness
Curiosity	Intuition	Timeliness
Decisiveness	Joy	Tolerance
Dependability	Justice	Trustworthiness
Determination	Leadership	Truth-seeking
Diligence	Love	Understanding
Discipline	Loyalty	Uniqueness
Discretion	Making a difference	Unity
Diversity	Mastery	Usefulness
Effectiveness	Obedience	Vision
Efficiency	Openness	Vitality
Elegance	Originality	
Empathy	Perfection	
Enjoyment	Positivity	
Enthusiasm	Practicality	

'From PE teacher to learning to code'

Libby was a secondary school PE teacher and now she's a software developer in early childhood education.

I love my work because it allows me to have a lifestyle that I want, freedom to do things like going surfing. Post Covid-19, I work more at home and am able to focus and concentrate on specific problems. I find it less stressful, and I enjoy writing code and solving problems.

After working in a summer camp in the States, I worked in outdoor education in the UK and France. I wanted to work with young people, and an opportunity to get into teaching presented itself when I returned to New Zealand.

I was teaching PE and some digital technology. The digital technology curriculum changed, and I upskilled by doing some coding courses. I did better than I thought, and I actually enjoyed it.

As a teacher, you're always thinking about the students and your teaching and never quite switch off. I knew I didn't want to teach PE for the rest of my life, and my wife didn't see enough of me either.

I have been in a number of roles where I have ended up not being happy, and it felt like it had got to the point where I just had to leave.

There were times when my stomach dropped and I thought, 'What the f**k have I done?' It was $10,000 to invest in my study, and it made me anxious at times to be making such a big career change.

I went from teaching secondary school to learning to code. My first software developer job was in the electricity industry, but I'm pleased now to be in a company that's education-focused. It makes more sense to me than electricity, and the company culture and values are more aligned to my own.

Where I choose to work tends to be about the people I get to work with and organisations that want to look after their people. The company I work for has a strong vision and great values. I enjoy the conversations I get to have about diversity and the things that matter to me. It feels like they have time for me.

My advice is to listen to your gut and go for it. For me, it's about doing something that makes you happy. (I acknowledge I come from a place of privilege and have not had as many obstacles to overcome as others.) When I make the decision, commit to it and put in the hard work, everything else seems to fall into place.

'I love helping people realise their goals'

Carissa is a project manager in a government organisation, working on delivering IT applications that help students, teachers and parents.

IT done well can streamline so many of our processes. I love helping people achieve and realise their goals. A lot of our projects are meaningful in some way, for example, an application that helps parents and schools apply for transport or funding to get kids to and from school. It's rewarding work and involved taking the current manual process and making it better by automating it and cutting down the time it takes.

Both my parents were in IT, and I thought IT sounded quite boring when I was growing up. I took a more creative route, including art school and interior design. I was in Melbourne with my parents after minor surgery and was quite bored, so I started helping them with their work and fell in love with it. I got a junior business analyst role, which involved understanding the needs and coming up with solutions. Now, in project management, I'm delivering those solutions from start to end, which is why I love it.

In my last role, I won employee of the year. It's so nice to be recognised and to know you're contributing to the company's success, and this helps you invest yourself in them and feel loyal. When I was new to project management, I took over a project which had been failing, at a time people were disillusioned, and I made it my mission to make people smile again and put in extra work to clean up what had gone wrong. It was a shame to see people having this experience around a project that could make such a difference, and improving their experience drove me to help them reconnect with the vision.

I look at a company's contribution to New Zealand; it's why I moved back from Australia, because I wanted to do the work I was doing for the betterment of my own country and people. I also consider working for companies based on their vision, ethics and work environment, the type of people they hire and the culture this creates.

My advice to others is to find a mentor and think about your ethics: what are you trying to achieve, and why are you here? What do you want to do with your life? What is it that motivates you? What gives you pleasure and joy, and how does this apply to the job you're doing?

Leveraging our strengths

Gallup surveys have found if we focus on our strengths, we'll be six times more likely to be engaged at work, 8% more productive and three times more likely to have an excellent quality of life. It's no wonder, given their data, they advocate for a strengths-based approach to career development.

It makes sense that when we talk about things we enjoy, it's also stuff we're good at. Work is more enjoyable when it aligns to our strengths. We also tend to perform better when we're doing things we're good at and using our skills.

NZ Stats found that those with a skill set that matched their job were more likely to be happy at work – 90% of those who said their skills were well matched were satisfied with their job.

Strengths are important, yet we ignore them in favour of talking about what we need to work on or improve where our career development is concerned. Strengths are be something we don't discuss or consider as much, even though they play such a vital part in our job satisfaction.

As a nation, we tend to err on the side of modesty. We can find it difficult or embarrassing to accept compliments; we are conditioned to be modest and not to promote our abilities through fear of being seen as arrogant. We struggle at job interviews because it feels foreign to 'boast' of our strengths and we're not used to selling ourselves.

Strengths can also be quite tricky because they feel effortless. If we're good at something, we tend to find it easy, so we assume it's nothing special, that everyone must find it this easy.

We have developed a tendency to focus on the negative. If someone were to give us two pieces of positive feedback and one piece of negative, it'd be the negative comment we'd remember and ruminate on, and we'd probably forget all about the positive things they said, even though they outnumbered the negative.

If it's effortless and easy (as strengths generally are), we don't think it's worthy of a mention. This combined with our concerns about boasting, not being modest or being seen as a tall poppy is a perfect storm for undervaluing our strengths.

We're also very good at focusing on our weaknesses. It's why our strengths don't come to mind so easily – we don't think about them, we're not aware of them and then we feel guilty/immodest for having them.

We are predisposed to focus on the things we're not good at rather than the things we are. We also emphasise this by spending a lifetime dwelling on this stuff and searching out evidence to prove ourselves right: we're not as good as people think, and there are some fatal flaws within us that mean we're not worthy and probably won't succeed.

Our brains are predisposed to think more negatively. It's how we've evolved and used to keep us safe. If we're constantly scanning the horizon for the worst that can happen, we are able to react and prepare for that, which helped us survive back in the days of sabretooth tigers. However, in our modern life, this translates to noticing all the things we don't like about ourselves, the things we've not done yet and what's not gone well for us at work.

If I ask you to think of one negative thing that's happened this week, it'll probably come quite easy. Something that didn't go well, someone who upset you? You'll have probably been thinking about it for days since it happened and ruminating on it at night. Now, if I ask you the same question about something positive, it's harder to recall; even if the positives outweigh the negatives for you this week, it's the negatives we remember and reflect on.

We're also very quick to move on to the next thing in our modern world so don't spend time reflecting on the positive, what went well, why, what strengths we used. It's about rewiring the neural pathways in our brain to see things more evenly. It's not that life will be any different; we'll just learn to see more of the positive as well as the negative.

Life has evolved at an amazing pace, and we've not caught up. Dr Barbara Fredrickson did some research on 'positivity ratios' and found to offset this bias that exists in the brain, we need a ratio of 3:1. That's three positive thoughts, emotions or experiences to every one negative.

There's a lot of work to be done in this space, as our negativity bias is like a well-worn walking track; we use it often. To even this out, we need to start firing more of the positive neural pathways and breaking down a less-travelled path in the brain. It's bumpy and overgrown with weeds so much more difficult to navigate.

It takes time, like training a muscle. We don't go into the gym and pick up the heaviest weight, and this is similar. It's not an overnight thing; we start small and build up – it takes practice.

Research has proven focusing on our strengths makes us more successful, but first we have to know what they are.

Stop for a minute and write down a list of your strengths – all the things you're good at. It may be your friends say you're a good listener or a good cook, or at work you've excelled in presentations or dealing with difficult customers. What feedback have you received at work? What did they tell you they'd miss about you when you left your last company?

Write a list, and take a moment to reflect on it and be proud of all the things you're good at.

My top five strengths are:

1. ....

2. ....

3. ....

4. ....

5. ....

Others tell me my strengths are:

1. ....

2. ....

3. ....

4. ....

5. ....

Ways these strengths play out:

....

....

....

....

....

....

Unfortunately, we are wired to spend more time thinking about what we're not good at than focusing on what we are. When we look at our goals and development planning, we tend to focus on our weaknesses and ignore our strengths. We think, 'That's already taken care of, so no need to spend time on stuff I'm already good at.' Or we overlook our strengths completely because we're just not well practised at celebrating our strengths, only worrying about our flaws.

Research has proven we reach our potential when we focus on our strengths, and it's something that takes less energy and is far more enjoyable. We're never going to be good at everything, and nine times out of 10, there are other people in the team who are good at the things we're not, and vice versa. The power of a team is in how we recognise our complementing skill sets and leverage our different strengths.

Roger Federer played both tennis and basketball growing up, and he was obviously very good at tennis. He chose to focus on this and leverage his strength, which eventually turned into his career, rather than focusing his time and energy on trying to get better at basketball. Yes, there are some weaknesses we may need to give some attention to, but overall, we achieve our potential by leveraging our strengths.

'Pay attention to what lights you up'

Cillín Hearns is a leadership and performance coach.

I love working with people. The variety keeps it interesting, because no two days are ever the same. Coaching, training, speaking, filming, meeting people and doing all the things that come with running a business. There's so much to it; I'm always stimulated.

I envy those who fall into what they should be doing and find their purpose in life at an early age – I didn't. I had no clue, so I've done many jobs as I meandered through my career, immersing myself in everything I tried.

A passion for sport and fitness led me to a fitness and leisure management course when I finished school. After that I worked as a fitness instructor and personal trainer and, through further study, treated sports injuries. I wanted to move into the information technology sector and so went back to university to study a BSc in Computer Science in the evenings, followed by a diploma in Corporate Management. Each time I changed my career, I'd go into it with enthusiasm, but after a few years, this would wear off and I'd be left unfulfilled, which led me to look for something else. It wasn't until I met a coach that I realised what I wanted to do; she really helped me tap into what was important to me.

I wasn't enjoying my job at that time, and whilst I was complaining to my wife one evening, she challenged me to quit and go out on my own. 'What do you mean? We've got the mortgage and kids. How can I just quit?' I said, but we worked it out and agreed to see how I went for six months. Despite my fears, I gave myself permission to give it a go, with the support of my family. I reminded myself if it didn't work out I could always fall back on what I was doing previously. Telling myself it didn't have to be forever gave me permission to experiment and try it out.

My coaching business built up over time, but in the beginning I fell flat on my face. There was a lot to learn, and I dipped back into the contract market as I was getting things off the ground. Slowly, the business grew to what it is today, but it was a lot of hard work and a lot of learning new things. Looking back on those years, I wouldn't go back and change any of it. I learned all the skills I have along the way and understand myself better; those experiences have helped to shape who I am today.

For anyone looking to find their 'one' thing, I recommend paying attention to the things that light you up – there are clues in there. I remember back in my personal training days, I loved learning, I always found myself mentoring others, and, on reflection, these were the things that lit me up.

A mistake I made in the past was when people would give me feedback and compliments, I would dismiss them as 'anyone could do that'. I didn't see that, in their eyes, what I was doing was really good. So pay attention to good feedback, because that's a clue that speaks to your skills and strengths. If you haven't found work you love, follow the things you're interested in. What books do you read? What lights you up in conversation? Explore what interests you; those things that draw you in are worth further investment of your time and energy. Have patience and be persistent. It doesn't happen overnight.

Chapter 3

Ways of working – the nine-to-five myth

WE'VE EXPLORED WHAT a job we love might look like, understanding what our skills and values are so this can fit with our work, and what purpose and impact might look like for us. Before we put this into action, let's pause and consider the final pieces of the puzzle: the impact of who we work with and, first, the way we do that work.

There are so many different ways of working, and flexibility continues to grow as our workforce evolves. Covid-19 has opened the door to flexible working and more home-based offices. No longer does flexible working mean parents who want to work part time and pick up the kids at 3pm. Flexibility is about hours, location and so much more. We're also not restricted to just one job anymore. Many people have a side hustle to supplement incomes or their sense of purpose.

Gallup has found a significant proportion of American workers have a non-traditional relationship with their employer. Twenty-nine per cent of all US workers have an alternative work arrangement as their primary job, and 36% participate in the gig economy. This refers to temporary positions where organisations hire independent workers for short-term commitments.

The Organisation for Economic Co-operation and Development (OECD) states that one in seven workers is now self-employed. Contracting and freelancing have become popular options, giving more freedom, variety and money for the same skills employers would traditionally employ people for. It also gives the employer flexibility to respond to seasonal peaks and market shifts.

This will continue to evolve, as work always has. The future of work is unfolding. Globalisation, digitalisation and other mega-trends are bringing radical shifts to how we live and work.

The world of work is changing. Artificial intelligence, automation and robotics will make this shift as significant as the mechanisation in prior generations of agriculture and manufacturing. While some jobs will be lost, many others will be created.

Technological progress, globalisation and ageing populations are reshaping the labour market. At the same time, new organisational business models and evolving worker preferences are contributing to the emergence of new forms of work. Whilst we might worry all our jobs are to replaced by robots, in actual fact, humans will always have a place and we've adapted and evolved already through many ages of the workforce since the industrial age.

Our working lives began out on the farms, on the land, in a manual way. Then the industrial age hit, and we worried we'd run out of food as people migrated into factories and production lines, machines and shifts became the norm. Then we moved from the industrial age into the IT age and moved into offices. A new way of working, the salaried age, was ushered in, and with it many factory workers wondering if they'd still be relevant. In all of these examples through the ages, we've adapted; we retrained and we evolved. Just as we are doing now with the automation age.

The media may have us believe robots are soon to replace us. To a degree, yes, artificial intelligence and automation will replace some of the jobs we do (approximately a third, it is thought). However, just as with the farming age, industrial age and information age, we will adapt and evolve – just like the farmers and the factory workers did. We'll retrain, and there will still be jobs; they might just look different. Our kids will be doing jobs we've never even heard of – a bit like my dad and my book-writing/speaking business!

Things have changed so much in the world of work just within a generation, and they'll continue to do so.

It makes me laugh when we talk to our parents about working from home. They struggle to comprehend how we can be both working and at home. It just didn't exist in their day. You either went to work or you stayed home. Well, what do you do if you're working at home? How do you work if you're at home?

It's not our parents' fault they don't get how we work these days. Just as I'm probably not going to understand the work my nieces and nephews will do. In fact, I'm already struggling to get my head around social media influencer as a career choice.

Gone are the days of 'a job for life', and, in fact, with the gig economy, we can now have lots of different jobs and roles at the same time: picking up contracts, working flexible hours, working for ourselves and working fixed term, part time for someone else.

Platforms like Uber, Airbnb and Fiverr are all enabling us to earn money without being employed.

Almost one in 10 New Zealanders has more than one job. Multiple job holders are also more likely to work non-standard hours, NZ Stats reports.

The opportunities are endless, which gives us so many more options when we're trying to map out a career plan that matches with our values, skills and aspirations.

In my parents' day, you were lucky to have a job, and you stayed in that job as long as you could. You were never supposed to enjoy it; that wasn't the point. I vividly remember at family parties all of my family comparing notes on how much they hated their jobs or their bosses and how much longer until they could retire, or when their next vacation was. This was just the way it was. Of course you needed a job to have a life, to put a roof over your head and feed your kids, and I'm forever grateful for the jobs my parents did that allowed me to have the life I had.

We were never well off, so my parents worked to gain the money we needed to cover the basics. There were times they'd have eggs on toast for tea so we could afford school trips. Dad would work in the day in manufacturing businesses, and Mum would go out and work at night in the hospitality industry when he came home. Then, when we went to school during the day, Mum worked in an office and Dad did shift work. It was tough but necessary to get by.

Times have changed, but for some, this is still a reality. The world of work has certainly changed. Gone are the job for life, the clocking in and out, and the nine to five in many places; gone is the five-day week too in some. We are expected to move jobs; lay-offs and restructures are commonplace and not just for companies downsizing.

We've become more innovative; organisational structures are flatter with less hierarchy. The way we work has evolved with the popularity of the agile and lean methodologies. Project teams that talk of scrums, sprints, stand-ups, war rooms and kanban.

Our offices have certainly changed, and what has also changed is our reliance on them and having our business revolve around set locations.

Covid-19 lockdowns across the world allowed us to explore a more fluid way of working. They enabled us to reduce our attachment to being in an office between certain times of the day, all stuck in the commuting traffic because we work the same times of the day.

They've led to businesses embracing flexible working, seeing productivity gains and reviewing the need for large, expensive office leases in city centres. People are considering moving to the countryside in the wake of less commuting and planning other things in their day that reduce the life-admin load at the weekends, because we can when we work from home.

Following lockdown in 2020, an Otago University study indicated 89% of New Zealanders wanted to continue working from home in some capacity and only 11% wished to return to the office full time. Perceptive backed this up with data suggesting 64% of us enjoyed working from home during lockdown and 46% of us believed we were more productive.

We enjoyed the fact there was no commute, therefore more time back and less stress (also saving money). Being undisturbed meant we could get more done and had more freedom to structure our day. People could adapt to work at their most productive times of the day. For some, this was earlier or later; there wasn't the pressure of being shoehorned into nine to five.

Being at home meant there was more time to be with family without guilt; this had a positive impact on wellbeing and relationships. We also noticed it was cheaper to make lunch and coffee at home than to buy it from nearby cafés. Tea breaks were with our nearest and dearest, not gossipy work colleagues or Jeff from IT. Working in comfy clothes, not office attire, was also a novelty for many.

Another surprising impact was we became more connected – albeit via a screen. For many businesses, the Auckland–Wellington office divide disappeared, because we were all in one big Zoom office. We felt part of a team and all in this together. That may also have been due to the impact of a global pandemic, but there was no mistaking that people checked in more and felt more connected being invited (via Zoom) into each other's homes, seeing their dogs and kids in the background.

What we saw from this home-based working lockdown experiment was some middle ground is preferable. People don't like to be at home all of the time. They miss the office, the structure and routine as well as the ability to separate home life from work life.

The collaboration and socialising with colleagues and the creativity and teamwork this breeds.

Regardless of our thoughts, Covid-19 has changed the way we work and the way businesses will approach workplace flexibility in the future.

Had this happened when I was still in the corporate world, would it have made a difference? I don't know, maybe. Perhaps I'd still be there now. The more flexible we make our work, the more people are likely to want to work for us and therefore the more skills and experience we retain in the business.

Pre Covid-19 and our new normal, many saw working from home as a treat, technically a day off. It was used as a reward and trust was a major issue. For decades, since the era of clocking in and out, bosses have liked the idea of knowing where their staff are, keeping an eye on them and making sure they're working during work hours – or at least present in the office.

The assumption was if we worked from home we'd all be busy watching Netflix, drinking tea and doing loads of washing instead. Then Covid-19 came along and we were all forced to work from home. And guess what? We still worked. We may have also done washing, drank tea and watched Netflix, but what bosses noticed was that productivity didn't suffer and employees could be trusted. In fact, many people reported working more, because they were up at the same time and didn't have the commute so found themselves logging on earlier than they would in the office.

Now, we may not always work as hard when we're at home, we may get distracted, we may be tempted to go to the gym in the middle of the day or take a longer lunch break to walk the dog or maybe even do the washing, but if we're getting the job done, does it matter?

It's like the concept of the four-day week, which was trialled initially in New Zealand in 2018 by Perpetual Guardian, an insurance company who asked its staff to take one day off a week (for the same, five-day-a-week salary). The trial was heralded a success and extended permanently following a 20% increase in performance and an increase in engagement, too, for both clients and employees. It attracted global attention and awards at the time, and founder Andrew Barnes went on to write a book about this flexible working revolution.

This experiment found that whilst we work one day less, we're actually more productive. Gone are the days when we're paid for every minute we're at the desk, clocking in and clocking out.

Of course, there will always be some people that take advantage, but these people are going to do this anyway, regardless of whether they're in the office or at home. So, yes, they might have spent half the day on Netflix and just wiggled the mouse to make sure Skype shows them as active. But put them in the office and whilst they'll be present, they'll also be chatting to colleagues in the kitchen, surfing Facebook and nipping out to the shops on non-work-related errands. To be fair, if people aren't pulling their weight or delivering, that's going to be the case whether they're in the office or sat at their kitchen table.

Presenteeism is the name used to describe this concept of being present at work in person but not actually engaged or productive. We might look busy, but we're not productive, or we might be sat at our desk but surfing Facebook.

The difference here is motivation, and when we're driven by purpose, doing something we enjoy and that we're good at, there's no temptation to fall into the presenteeism trap. In fact, it's not a happy trap to be in, it's one that's often boring and tiresome. Most of us would rather be doing work we enjoy than going through the motions of presenteeism to get paid.

The way we work has changed and is still changing. I sat down with Nick McKissack, CEO of Human Resources New Zealand, to talk about how work is changing and, of course, his views on loving Mondays.

'This year's pandemic has thrown up some challenges and opened up a whole new world of possibilities in terms of how and where we work and then how companies engage people in those settings. It's a new challenge for leaders to take the best of what we've learned and also figure out how we operate in this new world,' he said.

Nick made a valid point on the uniqueness of our Covid-19 situation. 'Lockdown was unique and not repeatable when we consider the novelty factor, the crisis factor and [the fact] we were all in the same boat. That created some positive attributes in a way, which helped us get through. The challenge is what can be carried forward as a positive and how we manage that transition.'

I asked Nick what he thought the way forward was and how the best companies he's seen have dealt with the task of engaging staff.

'Engaging with the people will help, as well as keeping the conversation going. Change poses some hard questions. Those who figure out how to incorporate this new way of being into the future will be the ones that are successful, and top talent will look for those organisations.

'Where I've seen engagement done well in organisations, purpose has been what's shifted the dial. There's been strong development and communication around vision and purpose, followed up with demonstrated commitment from the leadership team.'

But it's not all about our leaders, so what can we, the individuals within those organisations, do to take ownership and drive our own engagement? Nick's advice echoed my experience in my HR career.

'If we can give employees a sense that they own the difference they can make, it's much more enabling. Employees who feel like they are contributing towards something that means something have more ownership. I think purpose and autonomy to get the job done are two of the most important things.'

Nick told me, 'In my twenties, my boss told me, "Never let your manager make you less of a person than you are," and I really believe that. Even if you don't have a great boss, you can still find job satisfaction if you believe the purpose of what you're doing and have the feeling that you're making a difference.'

'I struggled to find the opportunity, so I created it for myself'

Maribel Aburto is co-founder of CREATIVA Design Studio.

I studied graphic design after I had my first child, then I studied web design. When we emigrated to New Zealand from Chile, trying to find a job in my field when English wasn't my first language was hard. I met Vera, my co-founder, and she was experiencing the same problems. We also needed something flexible to fit around the kids. It was difficult because we were in a new country and had few friends and no family support.

We had this idea, maybe we should do something together, so we founded a design studio, but we didn't think it would grow the way it did. It started because we struggled to find the opportunity we needed as professionals, so we had to create it for ourselves.

I love that I can do what I want, I don't have to ask for permission, I can try new things out. I fell in love with the person I became. I had no idea I had this ability to make this business successful and learn so much. I also enjoy the flexibility to work from home and take the kids to appointments.

My advice to others who want to start a business would be to try different things until you find what you love. A side hustle can help fund this and transit from your current job. Look for a mentor who is doing what you'd like to do and find out how they did it. Find your inspiration. Mindset has been key for me, and this has grown with my confidence as I have grown.

Now with CREATIVA we can create opportunities for others who are in the same boat. It started because of our own experience and struggles, and now we can provide flexible jobs to other women. It's our mission and vision to share our success and create opportunities for others who are experiencing the same struggles we had.

Chapter 4

The leadership impact

In *The 7 Hidden Reasons Employees Leave*, Leigh Branham says 89% of bosses believe employees quit because they want more money but in actual fact only 12% of employees leave for this reason. Most commonly people don't leave a job, they leave a leader, and there are still far too many leaders contributing to good people walking out of the door (often without even knowing).

Who we work with can have a huge impact on our job satisfaction, and none more so than those in positions of authority who we report to, who direct our work and who ultimately make decisions about our performance, autonomy and internal career progression.

A Careerbuilder.com study showed 58% of managers said they didn't receive management training. Most of us get promoted for being technically good at our jobs – the one we might have trained all our life for. We inherit a team, but when it comes to leading, so few are adequately trained for this.

Let me ask you who's the best leader you've had and why? What were the skills and traits they had?

They'll likely be competent in their job – that's why you respect them – but there'll be much more to it than this. In my workshops, common themes that emerge are very similar to what we outlined earlier when looking at what engages us at work.

Empathy, recognition, support, challenge, integrity, communication, calm, authentic, trust. They communicated so I knew what was happening and what they expected. They listened and valued my opinion. They didn't micromanage me but trusted me to get the job done my way. They had my back. They helped me grow and develop. They cared about me as a person.

These are all common responses to the question, 'What makes a leader great?'

It goes without saying, then, that a great leader will as a result of these traits also have a highly engaged team around them.

Whether it's a good manager or a bad one, they'll have an impact on the team – it's like the ripple effect when we drop a stone in a pool of water. Their traits, values, ways of working and expectations impact everyone around them.

If you are a leader yourself, consider this and the example you currently set in this space. A few of the fundamental elements of employee engagement, according to Gallup, centre around the type of leadership we have and support we get.

Simple acts like being cared for, being listened to and gaining recognition for a job well done are often so simple they seem too simple and are overlooked by many busy leaders. Yet the impact they have on employee engagement and performance is huge.

Global studies reveal 79% of people who quit their job cite lack of appreciation as their reason for leaving. People don't leave a job; they leave a leader.

We'll probably all have examples of great bosses we'd work with again tomorrow and those who've left us scarred for life!

Some we connect with; we may even have a laugh and joke with. They are people we'd hang out with out of work. Others are not so lucky. Regardless of what resonates most for you and your manager, you'll be wanting to manage the relationship, not just endure it.

We all know our boss manages us – it's how the hierarchy works – but we can also manage them. It's called managing up and a skill that, done well, can improve our relationships and aid our enjoyment at work. Simply put, it's about owning your relationship and being proactive in how you interact.

Leaders are people too, often under a lot of stress and not always on top of their own stuff (tired, busy or dealing with personal issues). They tend to struggle under pressure just like we do, and, as a manager, they're likely to be under more pressure as they take responsibility for the whole team; the buck stops with them. Some managers can feel out of their depth. If they are struggling or lacking in confidence, this can also present as poor behaviour or seeing you as a threat.

Regardless of their reasons, there's no excuse for poor behaviour, and when this steps over the line into bullying, you need to seek help and have it addressed – or leave. For some, even when they've spoken up, nothing changes and this becomes the only option, but I'd always advocate for saying something first and following the process many organisations have for protecting their staff when this issue arises. Trying to address the issues or at least ensure the individual can be aware of the impact of their behaviour and hopefully not inflict it on others in the future is the first step.

For most of us, it tends to be less extreme than this. We might not really see eye to eye, they're not great leaders, and it impacts on my happiness at work. They have good days and bad days like us all. Here are some tips to help make more of those days good ones.

Generally, if you're doing a good job, your leader will be getting credit and you'll be making their life easier. This is a good way of finding favour with the boss – great for your brand too.

Equally, knowing their buttons and when not to push them can help too. Knowing their working style and thinking preferences can help, including how they like to communicate.

If you work closely with your boss, you know when they are not in a great mood, save your question for tomorrow. You also know how a certain piece of news may be received and therefore the best way of breaking this. You know not to talk to them if their sports team has lost or if it's before 10am on a Monday morning, for example. Use this knowledge to your power in navigating your relationship with them.

If you have an opposing view, explain why and validate theirs too. 'That's a really good point. We might also want to consider [*your view*].'

Always stay calm, even when they are in a state of chaos or frustration. Set healthy boundaries in terms of your hours, how you work together, their expectations of you and how you're willing to be treated.

If you're going to them with a problem, make sure you've been proactive and thought about some possible solutions too. Make suggestions and offer your thoughts, then you can see if they agree and are happy to sign it off.

If something is unclear, ask for clarification, repeat back to them what you think they want you to do and ask clarifying questions to check for understanding. Not all bosses are good at making themselves clear or articulating what it is they expect of you.

Clear up any miscommunication and make sure you air any niggles or issues before they become big. Express your concerns, but do this in a positive way wherever possible. If you're frustrated about a concern, always wait until you've calmed down before having the conversation. It'll be so much more productive for both the outcome and your relationship.

What are their goals this year, and how do you play a role in supporting that? Acknowledge them and give them feedback. Ask for feedback too, so you get a better idea of their thoughts about you.

Keep them informed. No one likes surprises or to be blindsided – communication is key.

Don't take it personally if they're having a bad day; it's more about them than it is about you. They are human too.

Clearly, these tips work if you've got a boss who's reasonable.

We're not always that lucky. If you're being bullied or simply working for someone with misaligned values, then the best option is to change that and seek help and support to navigate this space. It can be one that impacts our confidence and ultimately our health.

Leadership isn't for everyone, and so often we're given the job before we've had the training or been adequately prepared. Our hierarchical structures generally mean if you're good at your job technically, you'll get promoted and eventually inherit a team of people and become a people leader.

Just because we're technically good at our jobs doesn't necessarily mean we'll also be great leaders or even want to lead a team of people. Consider if it's the right move for you and something you'd enjoy, and then ensure you're well equipped to step into that space. Leadership can be a rewarding career path, personally, professionally and financially, but it's not for everyone.

You may be comfortable rising to the top of your technical field as an expert without wanting to delve into the world of people leadership, and this is okay too. It's all about what works for you. Let's face it – our technical career is generally the one we're qualified in and have trained hard for many years to master.

'It was a calling for me; now I want to leave a legacy'
Orquidea is responsible for developing a national team of diversional and recreational therapists.
We deliver therapeutic recreation for older people living in care homes, so they continue to enjoy the things that give them meaning in life, and support them to enjoy leisure.
I love what I do because I get to see tangible results. I get to do a lot of coaching and mentoring with new recreational therapists and visit care homes and see the programmes being delivered, as well as developing training to help improve the work we do.

It's been a long journey from Mexico and international relations and human rights before I became a therapist in New Zealand. The high-level positions with government and internal affairs are fascinating, and I got to support people from a different point of view. But there are also a lot of barriers, and it's much harder to make a difference. It's a slower journey to seeing the fruits of your work and the impact.

Coming to New Zealand gave me the opportunity to explore different things. I've always had a passion for community work. It comes from my culture; we always support our elders until the day they die and are very community-minded. I began as a volunteer, working with children with disabilities, and it was natural for me to create programmes that led me to a full-time job and a scholarship to study. I worked in mental health and then eventually aged care, and that's when I realised – this is it! It was a calling for me, and now I want to leave a legacy.

It's not always been easy. I have been through bullying in the workplace and being told I'm worthless. I have experienced a group spreading horrible rumours about me to others; I felt humiliated. This was incredibly challenging but has made me stronger. The tall poppy syndrome has been a challenge for me too. I come from a culture where we celebrate success. I found people are not as keen to celebrate, praise or recognise each other.

The bullying undermined my confidence and impacted my health, but I decided I wasn't going to stand for it. What helped me was the support I had from friends and family. My husband tells me to take things only from people who've achieved things and know you, not from people who judge you or who've not achieved anything in life. I took more walks and got help from EAP (employee assistance programme), which I found really helpful. Doing coaching and mentoring is helpful, and asking for help, saying I'm not okay and seeking support, is key. It rebuilt my confidence and helped me feel empowered again. If you feel stuck, take some time and reboot yourself again.

Chapter 5

What should I do now?

By now you should have a good sense of what makes you tick: your strengths and values, as well as what you get out of bed in the morning for. This often leads to a realisation of what needs to happen next.

In this chapter we'll explore next steps and how to apply what we've learned so far. What does it mean and what do I do now? But first let's look at the possible reasons we might need to make a move and then – what might stop us!

Perhaps you've come to the realisation that it's your boss that's the problem, your company or the environment. Will flexible working cure your unhappiness, or a new department? Maybe it's a promotion that's required or a career change, or you're not quite sure yet but you know this job is not the one for you.

If this is the case, it's unlikely this is the first you've heard about it. It'll probably have been something stewing in the back of your mind for some time. A nagging doubt and a desire for change. It tends to hang out there for a while before it becomes actionable. That's good, though, because it gives us time to think, to process and sit with it to make sure it is the right call.

Hopefully the exercises here have helped you understand what needs to change and how to change it. It might be that there's nothing wrong with your job; it's the people around you, your boss or the company you work for. Maybe you'd be happy doing exactly what you're doing but elsewhere.

Or the opposite can be true. You love the people you work with, and your company has been good to you, but you just feel a bit bored. You've outgrown your current role and need more of a challenge.

Or perhaps it's bigger than that. Perhaps, like me, you've been climbing the career ladder for the last few years and only now you realise it was the wrong ladder. You've longed to do something that fills you with passion and excitement but have never really known what that is or that there's a choice beyond what you do now. After all, you've got a family and bills to pay.

Whatever your thoughts right now, sit with them and know the work we've done so far will help these next steps unfold.

It might be that you need a new challenge or a complete career change – you get to decide.

The awareness is always the first step, and this is a major step. It took me years of going back to what I knew before I realised it wasn't what I wanted, that I had to change. Once I sat with that, I was able to move into the next phase. That was working through the exercises we've covered in the first part of this book. Now we're on the edge of the cliff, ready to take a step into the unknown. It's exciting but also terrifying.

Getting to this point takes a lot of figuring out, but it's now that those thoughts and ideas turn into action. What action do you need to take, and how can that work for your personal circumstances?

It might mean budgeting the family finances, taking on extra shifts to pay for retraining or going part time to free up hours to pursue your next step. It might mean not taking a family vacation this year or remortgaging the house. It might mean signing up for a course, becoming a member of a professional association, enlarging your network, updating your CV or booking a meeting with a recruitment agency.

The options are endless; let's plan out yours. Start small, with little steps, and put a plan together for the next 12 months. I gave myself 12 months before any real action happened. That was time I could do the groundwork, set the ball rolling, retrain and educate myself.

The first thing to tackle will be all the reasons that might get in the way of your next steps. Now you know what you know and the change that's required, you might find you're stuck to the spot. Frozen in the face of fear or worried about what's next and the sacrifices this change might lead to – financial, status, the security of the familiar. But remember we've already identified this move will make us happy, and where we are is currently a place that makes us unhappy, so it's worth it.

Don't be disheartened if you need to sit with this for a bit. It took me years to summon the courage to leave my job and pursue my dreams.

There are a few things you can do to start the process before taking that leap of faith:

- Talk to your current company – your boss or HR – about the way you feel, what alternatives there might be or what tweaks can be made: other work, transfers, secondments, working patterns or issues with people that need to be resolved.

- Upskill – take some courses (there are many online), do some voluntary work, join groups and professional associations. Seek out more responsibility in your current job or get involved in other projects. Mix with different teams and gain a new perspective.

- Don't hang out with toxic co-workers or get embroiled in office gossip – it'll only make you more unhappy, and it does nothing for your brand either.

- Build your network – in person and online. Talk to other people about your plans, learn from the experience of others, listen to suggestions and get the word out you're considering a change or a move.

- Spend some time doing some self-reflection. The exercises in this book will help. It's critical you know yourself so you can make decisions aligned to who you are and what you want. If we don't know what we're looking for and what suits us, how do we know how to find it? Self-awareness is key in this space and will help align you with a career you love.

- Talk about how you feel and get help and support – from friends and family or, if it's appropriate, helpful colleagues. Get a coach or mentor; they can be useful not just in terms of bouncing ideas around but in helping you figure out a plan that gets you clarity and helps you bring this to life and make it happen.

- Start looking. This can be daunting but is also fun. Treat it as experimental research; it's just looking and assessing your options. Update your CV, search the jobs boards and talk to recruitment agents. This is a research phase, so you can do all of this and still stay where you are. You're not committing to making a move just by looking. But you might find the next move is ready and waiting for you.

- Develop other sources of income to give yourself more choices and flexibility. Consider the gig economy or some kind of side hustle based on your passions.

'Reinventing myself and experimenting'

Grant Verhoeven is a leadership and career development coach and trainer.

I love helping others ignite their talent, unlocking their potential through education and training. I enjoy helping people find work they love. My work fits with a lot of my skill set and my reason for being, my purpose. I get a kick out of giving this gift to others. I often think, 'I get paid to do this.' It's awesome, even though it's not without its challenges.

I got into career and leadership coaching through redundancy. I was working in fundraising and went through a redundancy consultation, an outcome of which was outplacement support. This was the first time I got some professional career coaching.

I wish someone had told me about it sooner, as it opened up my eyes to best-practice techniques to defining what I wanted to do and tools for getting there. It also gave me the confidence to launch out on my own, into something I had been thinking about for years.

I have worked for the past 10 years as a professional trainer, facilitator and coach. I run my own leadership and career development practice, focused on helping people get clear on what they want to do in their career and how to be the very best at work.

Prior to this I was the career consultant at Massey University, where I did over 700 sessions with students, helping them build their skills in networking, interviews, job-hunting, using LinkedIn and more. I found a way to help people going from total confusion to land on what they wanted to do or change.

One mistake I made was not speaking to people in the industry doing what I 'thought' I wanted to do. I was successful in landing a role straight from university to find I didn't enjoy it. I had a picture of the profession as one thing, whereas the reality was very different.

It was challenging reinventing myself, going from the marketing guy to training and coaching guy; we can have a lot of our identity tied up in our jobs.

My advice to others in this position is that there is a way to short-circuit the process of moving ahead in your career. Speak to people who have done it before, and realise there are people that can help you save time and pain in the process of career change or transition.

The road map I use in my coaching and training helps people follow this process and get clarity of what you're good at, what lights you up and who's going to pay you for it. Then you've got to test it like it's an experiment, to check it's right. Be open to asking for help and understand that clarity is the key to career fun and success.

Chapter 6

Why do we do
the job we do?

Whether you've decided to stay or go, these are big decisions and often not easy to make. It's advisable to sit with this and reflect before making a call. Decisions of this magnitude are often easier said than done, so it's important we understand how to navigate some of the fears and barriers that stand in our way. But before we understand how to overcome these barriers, let's look at why we choose to stay in the jobs we're in to start with.

There are many reasons we pick the jobs we do. Sometimes the job is secondary: it's because we want to live in that town that we do that job, or it's a stopgap for money whilst we save to go travelling. Maybe it's a part-time role whilst we bring up the kids or study to do something different. A stepping stone to get experience we'll need for our next move on the path to our dream job. It could be an opportunity to work with a friend who's hand-picked us for this new job, or starting a social enterprise.

There are so many reasons we pick a job. Sometimes these can be limited by our skill set, the town we live in, the market or our situation (hours of availability, physical health, if we can drive, if we have a criminal record, etc.).

Some of us find ourselves in jobs for our ego. We take jobs because they impress others or because we're told this is what success looks like. It's about the title, the status or the salary and benefits.

It says we're someone when we hand our business cards out.

Let's face it – one of the questions we get asked most often by strangers is, 'What do you do?' so it makes sense we have this pressure to make sure we can come up with an impressive answer. This can be the reason we're stuck in a job we don't enjoy, because it looks good and impresses others or makes us feel important.

I've worked in jobs I've loved just for the people I work with, others I've done just for the money, and some jobs I've done for free because I love the work so much and the sense of purpose I get from it.

Working behind the bar of my local pub was like being paid to chat to my friends; I loved it. Going to the office, though, not so much. I sometimes enjoyed the work, when it challenged me, but sitting in uncomfortable 'office' clothes in front of a computer under fluorescent lights and commuting in rush-hour traffic I detested. Back-to-back meetings talking about things that didn't really matter to me didn't fill me with joy. If I was honest, I was there for the money, so I could afford a nice holiday at the end of the year. But does it really make sense to spend 262 days of the year doing something I don't enjoy so I can afford two weeks living a life I do enjoy? Not when you put it like that!

I was also attached to the status and praise I got from others for my corporate job. The salary I earned and the privilege it afforded me. The meetings at posh restaurants and overnight stays in flash hotels. It made me feel like I'd made it – even though it didn't make me happy.

Working for free in voluntary roles at the SPCA cat wing, talking to the elderly at rest homes or teaching English to Buddhist monks – these were my most rewarding jobs, but I wasn't being paid, so why?

The sense of purpose, the freedom of choice and the ability to give back and get out of bed for a purpose – this comes when we can see what we do helps, that we're needed and we're doing good for the world. It also teaches us a lot.

There's often an intrinsic motivation at play that can be far more important (and rewarding) than the extrinsic we've given prevalence to for so long. But we don't always see it, even when we're desperately unhappy at work and dreading each Monday morning as it rolls around.

We've looked at why we do the jobs we do, but if we're unhappy, why is it that so many of us stay in our jobs?

Why don't we leave?

Regardless of the reason we're unhappy at work, if any of the above resonates for us, shouldn't we just quit? Why don't we leave?

Most of us in the developed world are not forced to be there. We have a choice and can leave at any moment, so why don't we?

It's not that easy. So many factors play into this big decision. The most obvious being money. I need this money to survive, especially if I've got responsibilities, bills, rent, kids. I can't not have an income. I've got debts to pay. What if I don't get another job? There are not enough jobs in the market to risk it right now. These are some of the common reasons we stay put.

They'll also be lots of other factors that stop us. Our own fear of the unknown, not being confident we can make the change. Not wanting to lose what we've got and the security of the familiar. The career we've put so much effort into already. What will other people think? I like my colleagues and I'd feel bad for leaving them in this mess.

This can be especially true if it's a career change – I don't want to have to start at the bottom again. This is all I know and what I'm qualified for. It's familiar, but also wouldn't it be a waste of a decade if I now decided to do something different and start again?

There's also a sense of pressure we can often feel that stops us. This can come from inside ourselves or externally, from friends, family, colleagues or society. I've put too much into this career to give up now, what will people think, everyone else is doing it, my parents are proud, my friends think I'm successful, I earn good money, my colleagues respect me, who am I if I'm not my job title?

These are certainly all things I've said to myself and have stopped me moving forward at times. When I left the corporate world and my well-paid job, with its senior status and top-of-the-range company car, I noticed a bit of my identity went too. Especially given I was unemployed and living in yoga ashrams, cleaning composting toilets. I was happier than I'd ever been, but was I still successful? Did I still feel important, and would people respect me the same way?

But surely success is being happy – they can't be two separate things, so let's not treat them as if they are. Many 'successful' people admit to being unhappy. In my opinion, we're not successful at life until we're also happy.

What about the fear of the unknown or not having another alternative? Perhaps the reason we won't leave is because we don't know what else to do – this was true for me for many years.

This was all I knew, and I didn't have a plan B. I didn't know what my new bright shiny career or dream job looked like, so how could I possibly find it? I decided to stay with what I had until I'd figured out the alternative – that never happened.

What happened instead was the pain of being where I was got too much to bear and I had to take a leap before I'd figured out the next step. But in taking the leap, I was able to figure out the next step. I had the time and energy to start rebuilding my career around my passions.

Even worse than the fear of the unknown is this: what if we do have an idea of an alternative but we get it wrong? What if we fail?

Many of these reasons we've discussed boil down to one very simple yet impactful factor – FEAR.

Fear and our comfort zone

When was the last time fear stopped you? Fear can leave us frozen to the spot, and it stops us moving forward. Much of why we resist change or doing something new is because of fear. Fear of what people will think of us, fear of the unknown, fear of losing what we have, fear of rejection and fear of failure.

But is fear always a negative? And how do we learn to navigate it, embrace it and, ultimately, overcome it so it doesn't stop us from achieving our potential?

When I was growing up, fear kept me alive. Not walking down a dark alley late at night because of *that feeling*, making sure I looked before I crossed the road, checking the harness before I did the bungee jump, moving away from the edge of the clifftop on a windy day – I guess I have a lot to thank fear for.

But then, it's also the reason I spent too many years stuck in a life where I didn't belong. It was because of fear I spent years in a career that suffocated my soul and struggled to leave a relationship I'd outgrown.

Our fear of failure is what keeps us frozen to the spot; a fear of rejection means we sometimes won't even try. But why do we fear rejection and the answer 'no' when often we've nothing to lose?

No is our starting point, no is the answer if we don't ask, so why not ask the question? Asking is the only way we change the no into a yes, and perhaps there is a risk we don't get a yes, but then we're still back where we began in the first place – at no.

We can fall, and we can fail, but it's about how we learn to get back up, carry on and grow into the people we are capable of being.

When we get out of our comfort zone, take risks and give it a go, one of two things will happen. We'll either succeed, and that's great, or we'll fail and learn something that'll help us succeed at some point in the future, when we try again.

Both paths can lead us to success. Just because we might fail once in a while doesn't mean we should stop; this is evidence not of our incompetence but merely that we needed to learn something to help us develop our competence.

> 'Failure should be our teacher, not our undertaker. Failure is delay, not defeat. It is a temporary detour, not a dead end. Failure is something we can avoid only by saying nothing, doing nothing, and being nothing.'
>
> —*Denis Waitley, The Psychology of Winning*

This was true for me with the events I started to put on when I first arrived in Wellington. I knew nobody, the events were free and sometimes no one showed up. I could have taken this as a sign of failure and stopped trying, but I knew I had a lot to learn about marketing and a reputation to build in a new city. I learned what I needed to know and continued to show up, and four years down the track, I sell out venues.

I used to think to be successful, I had to avoid failure – surely this would mean success by default. I now know this is not the case, and it's changed my relationship with failure. I see it now as something inevitable and therefore expect it and embrace it.

After all, failure is how we learn and grow; it's a step closer to success, and it's part of the path we must follow. Those who've 'made it' have failed, learned and tried again until they've succeeded.

The first thing I did when I left my corporate job was train to be a yoga teacher. Now, that's not become my new career, as much as I enjoy it. Was that a failure or just a detour down the path to success which ultimately landed me this job?

Bestselling authors can release sequels that flop, sporting superstars can have bad games, and the most capable people can make mistakes. There are seasons to our souls. Some days, we are at our best, and everything flows, and we achieve great things. Other days, we can do exactly the same, yet the results don't turn out how we planned.

Every failure takes us a step closer to success. Ask yourself, 'What is this trying to teach me? What can I learn?'

It's taught me to see the success in failure – not just the lessons learned, but the small wins along the way. At the times when I've not been making money, this has allowed me to focus on getting emails from followers saying what I've said has inspired them in some way. This is a success in my eyes.

Those who have succeeded and those who we aspire to be – it's not that they've done it right and we're doing it wrong. They've already weathered the storms we're in now.

They've got to be where they are through the failures along the way. They've learned lessons, got back up and turned it into success.

Don't let fear of failure stop you even trying. And if you do fail, so what? It's a step closer to success, it's a lesson learned, and it's part of the path to grow into the person you're capable of being. Even the best fail, and this is *why* they succeed.

Taking the leap

But how do we know now is the right time to take that leap? Often fear keep us waiting, but there's also an element of procrastination here too – the feeling of not quite being ready yet.

I'll just wait until I've got a bit more money, until I've got another qualification, until I've lost 5kg, until after my holiday. There's always a reason to put it off. Often we're waiting for conditions to be perfect before we begin.

If we wait until we're ready or for perfect conditions, we might wait forever. In our minds we're never ready, even when we're beyond ready. This is particularly true when we think about taking a risk, getting outside our comfort zone – we'll never be ready to face the fear because we're waiting for the fear to dissipate, and of course it doesn't until we give it a try.

If it's a job, we'll always think we need a bit more experience or an additional qualification to be ready. The irony is if there wasn't a stretch or challenge in the role and we could do it from day one, we'd be incredibly bored.

We also like to have certainty, and this can be what we're waiting for. We might want it all mapped out and to see all the possibilities and know this is the right path before we set off. If we know exactly where this is heading and where we'll end up, maybe then we're ready to take the leap. But the saying is true: you don't always need to see the whole staircase to take the first step.

I had no idea what my new career would be when I left the corporate world and went down many paths, trying new things. Sometimes the path only emerges as we travel along it.

It's called our 'comfort zone' because it feels nice, safe and comfortable, and that's why it's so easy to stay there.

It takes courage to step outside our comfort zone and do things that are different and unfamiliar. But if we can move outside our comfort zone, it expands, and as our comfort zone becomes bigger, we learn more. Things become easier because there are now fewer things outside our comfort zone and therefore less that scares us.

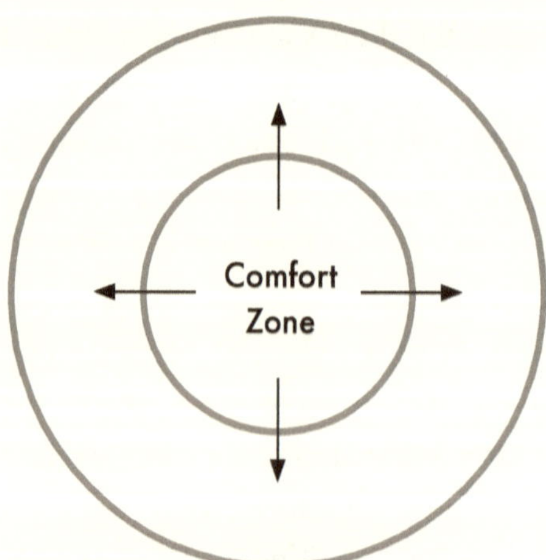

I use public speaking as an example because it sits outside of most people's comfort zones, mine included.

Because I've spent years as a speaker, people think it's something I'm naturally good at, something I wanted to be.

The truth is I was an author first. I'm an introvert, and sitting by myself, writing books, was my comfortable place. Then I started to be asked to speak about those books, something I'd never planned and initially filled me with fear.

Public speaking sits outside of most people's comfort zones, and when we have to do it, generally it's unpleasant. Our voice wobbles, we shake, we get butterflies and our palms sweat – this was certainly true for my first few times.

We also worry hugely when people watch us, when we put ourselves out there, because we might fail or we might mess up, we might make a fool of ourselves and we worry what people will think.

The funny thing is, though, the more we do it, the more comfortable it becomes and the better we get at it. Our competence starts to help us feel more confident, and those nerves dissipate.

For the first year of speaking, I couldn't hold a microphone because my hands shook so much; these days, that's not the case. Put anything else in the place of the public speaking example and the principles are the same. We feel the fear and it may be hard initially, but competence breeds confidence and practice makes its better. Our comfort zone then expands to now include public speaking or whatever example you use in its place.

It's a critical part of navigating our comfort zone and facing fear to step outside – this is the only way we develop, grow and challenge ourselves to unlock our potential.

It's always going to be fearful getting outside of our comfort zone, and there's always a bit more time or experience required to get it perfect and be 'ready', but sometimes we just need to lean in, say yes and take the opportunity.

Change is possible, even though it can also be terrifying. We don't always know what we want to do from leaving school, we don't always end up in jobs that are aligned to who we are – but we do get the chance to learn along the way and ultimately change that, as many of these people we'll hear from now have done.

Career success stories from others

Celebrity DJ Calvin Harris worked at a fish farm to fund his DJ side hustle in the early days.

Sean Connery had an array of jobs before he found his passion for acting, including milkman, ditch digger and lifeguard. Kanye West was a store assistant at GAP and Nicole Kidman a massage therapist. All jobs they earned money in before they found their passions, which they obviously now make a lot of money in.

But what about those who are not so well known? Those who are not famous for their careers but love them regardless? Here are three stories from people in New Zealand who've changed course for a variety of reasons and at various stages of their careers and found a jobs they love.

'I wanted to do more than earn good money'
Jennifer Young is the founder of workplace wellness and development consultancy Intentional Generations.
I have two main motivations. Firstly, my older brother, Alex, died at 10 years old due to brain cancer. His short life serves as a personal reminder to make the most of every day and has motivated me to do something greater than myself that leaves a positive impact.
Secondly, I know what it's like to feel lost and to be so badly impacted by the work environment your own wellbeing and mental health suffer. I experienced in my first professional role after graduating a culture so toxic many of us were

negatively impacted. My confidence got crushed and I developed high-functioning depression and anxiety to the point of having panic attacks and experiencing suicidal ideation. I never want another person to go through what I did, and this gives me the drive to do what I do now.

Initially, I studied law and was on track for a well-respected career and traditional life path. A turning point occurred when I had three weeks left of the course I was doing (which is the final training before being admitted to the High Court as a lawyer/barrister and solicitor). An email came into my inbox with an opportunity to do a 21-day Outward Bound course on a full scholarship. I immediately talked to my course organiser, as this was a once-in-a-lifetime opportunity. Luckily, I could re-enrol and finish the final law course with a different cohort. This was one of the best decisions I've ever made. This Outward Bound experience was the first time out I'd had by myself to investigate what it was I actually wanted to do since I'd entered university.

I realised I wanted to do more than earn 'good money', write contracts and represent clients. I knew I wanted to do something that gave back and helped people, but I didn't know what that looked like. This time away helped me explore this, alongside the coaching and mentoring I was getting. Seeing the impacts of getting outside of our comfort zones at Outward Bound ignited a passion in me to explore coaching, leadership development and wellbeing.

One of the best pieces of advice I've ever received came from a senior leader I met at a leadership development programme. He advised me, 'Take the time to figure out what you want to do: your mission and vision, the kinds of people you want to be working with, the ways you want to work and who for. You don't want to end up like me …

I'm in my fifties, my kids hate me, I'm getting a divorce, I've got a huge mortgage, I feel stuck and I'm miserable.' I took this advice on board and spent a significant amount of my spare time reflecting on this, taking different self-awareness assessments, doing 'coffee interviews' with people I admired, volunteering to learn different skills and figuring out for myself what advice I wanted to follow.

Now, I wake up and think, 'Wow, I get paid to do this.' Even on the busy weeks, I love what I do. I get to spend time supporting interesting humans, training inspiring leaders (including youth at high schools), working in organisations and doing coaching, workshops and webinars. I'm privileged to share my knowledge and experiences every day in ways that positively impact individuals and their wider communities. At the end of the day, I feel proud of myself for taking the leap to make all of this happen.

My advice to others is only you know yourself and your dreams. You know yourself better than your friends, family and societal expectations. The more you ignore your inner knowing of what you're here to do, the louder it tends to get – this was true for me. I ignored the voice that 'something wasn't right' for so long it negatively impacted my mental health and wellbeing. Through challenges, I've learned that your wellbeing, happiness, sense of purpose and connection to others is the most important thing. Building your own dreams and doing work that makes you feel alive is so much more important than listening to society's expectations.

'There's always someone who needs what you've got if you're good at what you do'
Angela is Executive Director of People and Capability, working in education.

I believe what I do makes a difference, and I work for an organisation that makes a difference in New Zealand.

I went to university studying social work and physical education with the intention of becoming a police officer, but I failed the medical. I was devastated and went travelling. I looked at where I could earn the most money to fund my travel, and this was IT. I was a project administrator to start, but I was always drawn to showing people how to use the systems and training them.

I sat specialist exams, became a certified Microsoft trainer and got my people fix through the classroom, and this developed into instructional design and online courses. The missing piece for me was the strategic view – how did I know what I was doing was going to make things better for the organisations I worked with? I was in the banking sector, which I felt was more about growing market share and selling more products. I was fortunate enough to be restructured out, which ended up being liberating.

In the past, I've left roles because I've been frustrated by leaders who are great at their jobs but not great at leading people. I also remember working long hours and trying to read the shortest bedtime stories possible to my kids so I could get back to work. It was then I knew I had to leave.

My advice to others is to find someone who can talk about your future with you: a peer, friend, mentor or family member. Knowing there are future possibilities reduces the feeling of being trapped in a role that isn't fulfilling and ultimately leads to creative and innovative thinking. There's always someone who needs what you've got if you're good at what you do, with the right intentions. Talk to others, and they just might know someone. Talking about the possibilities of what could be helps us feel less trapped. Give yourself a litmus test at the start of a role – why am I here, and what's my purpose? – and don't lose touch with that.

'I was always meant to work with people'

Janice is a learning and development manager.

My role is focused on finding those development opportunities people can use to do their job better and future-proof their skills. I am privileged to watch people develop and progress through their career, and playing a small part in this is incredibly rewarding.

I've always loved working with people. When I left high school, I wanted to be a psychologist, so that's what I studied. My work-experience days were days I didn't enjoy; it carried such an emotional strain. It made me realise despite the seven years of study, this was not the right job for me.

My first experience of learning and development came through teaching people how to use computers and being an IT software trainer. I didn't get the buzz from staring at numbers and formulae all day; this led me to change. I sought out what I was enjoying about my job and it was being with people, not the coding and number crunching I did in solitude.

So I decided to take a sideways step, to go to a more people-focused role, and the light-bulb moment happened – I was always meant to work with people. I knew this was the right step for me, even though it was fixed term so a risk and not the salary I was used to earning.

I really like the people I work with. My team are supportive, and from joining I was welcomed warmly, like I was part of the family. Trust plays a very big role in our team. I'm usually very planned and organised; however, my work can be quite reactive, so my day rarely goes to plan. Because I love what I do, I can see beyond a bad day or when things don't work out. One of the most enjoyable parts of my role is getting out from behind my desk and meeting people. I enjoy sharing stories and getting to know them on a personal level to understand what's going on in their world too.

I get involved in everything; my job is varied and covers more than just learning and development. My psychology study has put me in good stead and my skills get used a lot to build relationships. I'm not the kind of person who says, 'This isn't in my job description.' I'm keen to learn, always ready to help out, muck in and make it happen. This has left me open to more opportunities that have come my way. My advice to others is to do a full stocktake to discover what drives you, what your strengths are, what interests you and makes you happy. Find your why and look at what resources you have available to make it happen – your room for movement. Can you relocate, can you survive on a lower salary? Sometimes, when we're forced to, we realise we can actually do the things we've previously excluded.

Test your ideas and options out before taking the plunge. Use opportunities like volunteering, coaching or mentoring programmes to help you find the job you will love doing.

Chapter 7

Preparing for your next job

REGARDLESS OF WHETHER you've read enough already and have written out your resignation letter or you're still gathering the pieces of the plan for your next career move, this chapter will help you do that.

Once we know our strengths, our values and how we want to use those to make a difference in the world, we're halfway there. Whilst dealing with the barriers, fears and other challenges that might stand in our way, the next step is preparing ourselves to make a move.

This could be career progression or leaving our current role or even our entire industry as we navigate a career change.

In this chapter, we'll look at preparing for that move, including our CV, the job-interview process and negotiating a new job offer, ensuring we pitch ourselves at the right level and gain the confidence to put our best foot forward.

Believe you can!

When you've been comfortably employed for years, it can be daunting looking for a new job or entering a competitive market, making the step into the unknown to start your own business or contemplating a career change that makes you feel like a novice, starting from scratch again.

We've talked about the impacts of fear and taking a step into the unknown, but another barrier can also be our self-belief.

Fortunately, preparing for a new job can be a great way of boosting this and revisiting the evidence of our capability. Updating our CV, writing down our achievements and preparing for an interview to sell ourselves all have positive impacts on our self-belief.

It's quite normal to look at a position for a new job and not tick all the boxes. Does this mean we're not ready for the job? Not as often as we think. It means there are things we have to learn. Let's face it – if we ticked all the boxes on the job description, we'd likely be bored by week two of the new job. We want a challenge; we want to learn and grow. Our transferable skills and our ability to learn bridge this gap, so if you're looking at your next career move, thinking, 'I've never done that,' add 'yet' to the end of your sentence.

Beyond the obvious qualifications and experience requested on the job specification, it's not that we can't do it, it's just something we've not learned yet.

Whilst we talk about self-belief and common feelings of insecurity that arise when changing jobs, we need to consider the common barrier of imposter syndrome.

'Imposter syndrome' is a term describing high-achieving individuals who are marked by an inability to internalise their accomplishments and a persistent fear of being exposed as a 'fraud'. It's a voice of self-doubt that, despite our successes, keeps us feeling like we might fail, we might not be good enough and we might get found out.

We're constantly striving but always feeling like we're falling short, worrying we're not enough. That to be successful we have to be more, better, improved in some way.

It takes us away from the skills we have, the things that make us amazing and the success we achieve along the way. It breeds self-doubt and this feeling we're overrated by others because we don't feel as good as we need to be to hit the mark.

According to a 2011 International Journal of Behavioral Science review, 70% of people think they're not as good as others believe they are. This has been termed imposter syndrome, imposterism or imposter experience.

It's particularly prevalent at work and especially when we're taking on new challenges, a new job or a promotion. When we're feeling vulnerable or like we've got a lot to learn, it's common to have this voice pop up and say, 'Are you this person, can you do this, are you sure they've got this right?'

When I deliver my imposter syndrome workshops, there's always someone in the room hearing it for the first time, and I see a lightbulb go off for them, the same way it went off for me. 'This is a thing, it has a name, it's not just me.' There's a lot of power is this realisation.

The irony is we are generally good at what we do if we're having these doubts about our ability. 'Sure, I'm successful, but I can explain all that. It's just because they like me, I was lucky, I have a great team, actually, it's nothing and anyone could do it, maybe there's been a mistake.' Does any of that sound familiar?

Those with imposter syndrome have a tendency to attribute their success to external factors – like luck, or the work of the team.

Now, there's nothing wrong with sharing credit where it's due, but not at the expense of yourself; that's self-sabotage.

Imposter syndrome is not something we overcome; rather, we navigate it as it appears in our life. It may always be there but have varying degrees of impact on us, depending on how loud we turn the volume up. It can be different at various times of our life or in different areas of our life.

Check below and take the test to see if you've got imposter syndrome.

I find it hard to accept praise	
I focus on the things I'm not good at rather than my strengths	
I think people overrate me and worry they'll find out I'm not as good as they think	
I often succeed despite being convinced I'll fail before I begin	
I tend to think those around me are better	
I hate asking for feedback	

The more of the above apply, the more likely it is imposter syndrome is at play.

It can feel like we're the only ones experiencing this, as it's not often talked about, particularly in the workplace. Let's face it, it's pretty career limiting to admit to our boss or peers that we don't think we're as good as they do! So we're left feeling like it's a character flaw in us, further evidencing these feelings of imposterism.

However, we're not alone; many people experience imposter syndrome, especially high achievers and even those we look up to and aspire to be. Celebrities we assume are successful superhumans freely admit to feeling this self-doubt despite their successes. Jodie Foster said when winning her Oscar she thought they'd made a mistake, that someone would come and take it back and tell her it was actually meant for Meryl Streep. Whilst Meryl Streep told *USA Weekend*, 'Why would anyone want to see me again in a movie? And

I don't know how to act anyway, so why am I doing this?' Successful stars like Serena Williams, Tom Hanks and Michelle Obama, and even New Zealand Prime Minister Jacinda Ardern, all admit to feelings of imposter syndrome.

Imposterism can force us to play it safe to avoid failure and work twice as hard to prove ourselves and not get 'found out'. We might not apply for the promotion in case we fail, or put our hand up at that meeting to ask the question in case it's a stupid question.

Each time we *fool* people into thinking we are as good as they think, we increase the pressure on ourselves. If we get the promotion or pull off that project, rather than seeing evidence we're capable, our imposterism will have us think, 'Thank God I didn't get found out that time. Now I'm going to have to try even harder not to get found out.'

It's an exhausting act, to the point where sometimes we might wonder, 'Is it worth it?' A lawyer I was coaching once said to me, 'My local café is advertising for a barista, and I'm seriously thinking of applying. At least then I'll know I'm capable, my job will be easy and I won't have these constant feelings of inadequacy every day.' She was a hard worker and a high performer but also plagued by imposter syndrome.

Sadly, it's not something we can easily overcome – but we can learn to navigate it and succeed anyway. Here are some top tips to help:

1. Own your successes

You didn't get lucky; it wasn't by chance. We tend to be modest when it comes to our achievements, and have been brought up not to boast about our strengths. We feel uncomfortable accepting praise, and the negativity bias in our brain means we're wired not to think of the positives so much.

We dismiss other people's claims in this space and reason

they're just being nice because we've convinced ourselves we're not deserving of the praise. We put it down to luck, and, yes, sometimes there might have been an element of that: a place at the right school, the right person reads your blog and elevates it, you become a last-minute replacement on a big stage, you know the right people. But it doesn't make you any less deserving. Luck might open the door on the opportunity, but your capability allows you to walk through the door and make a success of it.

Bill Gates was gifted his first PC, that was the opportunity, but I'm sure many others had similar opportunities they didn't turn into Microsoft. The most important thing to remember is if we're getting praise or positive feedback, it's because *we've earned it* and deserve it. Own it and let it help counter some of those moments of self-doubt. If all you can say in the face of this is 'thank you', it's a lot better than anything that'll downplay it or wave away the acknowledgement.

2. Give it your all and know it's enough

Sometimes our imposter syndrome is due to our fear of failure and this fear of not being good enough. We fail to meet our own unrealistic ideals of perfection – in either the way we look, our abilities in life or our achievements at work.

No one is brilliant 24/7, although we put pressure on ourselves to be. We're not on top form all the time, but because we're capable of brilliance, we expect it all the time, and then beat ourselves up when we fall short of brilliance on our off days.

Overcoming imposter syndrome requires self-acceptance: we don't have to attain perfection to be worthy of the success we've achieved. We don't have to be Einstein to be a valuable asset. Nor do we have to attain perfection to share something with the world.

3. Don't let doubt and fear stop you

We need to continue to take risks and challenges even though we might not think we're ready. Too often, we stand back and let the opportunities pass us by because we doubt our abilities. The best way to see if you're ready is to dive in and take on the challenge.

There will always be a feeling of fear and the risk of failure – we grow and develop by facing these fears and getting outside of our comfort zone. Don't let worries hold you back. Growth is supposed to be uncomfortable; it's a sign we're being challenged and stretched, and that's how we learn.

The trouble is the higher we go, the further we have to fall, and this increases our sense of fear and our imposter syndrome as we climb the career ladder.

One of the ways we can navigate these feelings is by proving we're capable. This capability brings with it confidence and lessens the power of self-doubt, increasing our comfort zone and our confidence by proving we have the competence and capability.

4. Acknowledge it and know it's not just you

We need to be mindful the voice in our head is often swayed. We are wired to see the glass as half empty, to focus on the negative. This comes from evolution, back in times when it was helpful for us to scan the horizon for the worst that could happen in order to survive.

What this can translate to in our modern world is a constant focus on what we're not good at, things that went wrong, and why we're not enough. To counter the bias, we need to focus on what we have, not what we haven't, to direct our energy towards the things we're good at rather than what might go wrong and where we might fail.

Know this is not something we experience alone. Some of the most successful people I know who seem to have mastered life admit that underneath, they feel the opposite some days. Even famous people earning millions and excelling at what they do admit to having moments of self-doubt.

5. Stop comparing yourself to others

It's the fastest way to feel inferior and feed our self-doubt. Unfortunately, there will always be someone more qualified, clever, talented or strong than you. However, the reverse of this is also true. So instead of comparing yourself to others, look to see if you're fulfilling your own potential and celebrate the things you have.

We are all capable of more than we know, and we can do amazing things if we're not busy doubting our abilities. Next time the negative voice in your head starts to speak, turn down the volume.

What matters most is not whether we fear failing, looking foolish or not being enough; it's whether we give those fears the power to keep us from taking the actions needed to achieve our goals.

Setting yourself up for success

Once we have the belief and confidence to take a step forward, we need to ensure we're prepared.

Nick Roberts is CEO of Momentum Recruitment. We sat down and spoke about what it is people look for in their jobs, who the best companies to work for are and what makes us love what we do.

'Historically, the main driver has always been key competencies and skills, but now cultural fit is key,' Nick told me. 'We want cultural fit but also a person who's going to bring diversity and inclusion and add different thoughts and opinions.

'We see different views on this through the generations. Previously, we looked for stability and career progression, whereas now people are open to working for 10 different organisations and in a very different way.

'Covid-19 has also contributed to how we work and what we look for in work, particularly with the trust required for working remotely. Trust is hard to gain but easy to lose. Candidates are looking for this as well as flexibility, working for the right company, the leadership styles, the growth and opportunity as well as money.

'Popular companies to work for tend to have great cultures and have things like integrity, honesty, transparency and collaboration at the heart of their values. Companies who can motivate and inspire you as well as make you feel trusted and safe. Those who are given autonomy and gel with their teams tend to love their job; they have a sense of belonging with their work families.

'Feeling supported and the human element to our roles are fundamental to the environment at work and therefore our happiness whilst we're there. Our biggest need is to be valued and see we're making an impact. Adding value and making a difference is what fills our cup.

'I've made mistakes and moved just for money or a perceived career opportunity. Getting advice from others is helpful, having mentors or someone you can bounce ideas off. Some people might have a wish list and criteria to follow about the kind of role, organisation and leader they want to work for, thinking ahead strategically about their career. Others can make more of a snap decision because it's their nature.

'Fear can play a big role in why we choose not to leave a job even if we're unhappy. Change can be difficult, or sometimes we think the grass is greener and it's not. When we lose candidates, often it's due to a counter-offer, for either more responsibility or more money.

'Typically, we see those people come back to market six to 12 months down the line, though, because the things the person was looking for previously are still there, whether it's a change of industry, a new boss or better communication; the frustrations will still be there.

'For those preparing to make a move, I advise knowing what you want and tailoring your CV accordingly. Unless your chosen career is in demand because there's not enough of you, you're likely to be competing with other candidates. Consider the best way of presenting yourself. Taking the time to call or meet for coffee in this digital age helps keep you front of mind or be more than a statistic or number. A lot of recruitment systems these days have algorithms that sort through shortlisting because of the volume. Without knowing the people personally or having introduced yourself, you become a statistic the system will sort through.

'Cover all the skills and competencies that relate to the role you're applying for and have them in order; this boosts your chances of the algorithm matching you to the job. But also know those hiring so they can put a face to the name and know you beyond the percentage match the system gives you.'

Nick offers some sound advice, straight from the coalface. Let's look at the importance of your employment brand, and then we'll get into the detail of preparing your CV and readying yourself for the job interview. But first, make sure you don't overlook those transferable skills you bring and the experience that makes you feel 'good enough' and ready for your dream job.

We have many skills that are not on our CVs yet are transferable to so many workplaces. We need to think outside the box when comparing our skills and experiences for promotions or new jobs. Things like project management, conflict resolution, motivating others, budgeting, building relationships and communication are skills most of us have mastered before we've even set foot in the workplace – especially if we've brought up children.

We consider *leader* a formal title and a managerial position, yet, in reality, leadership comes in many forms, inside and outside of work. It doesn't just mean a title or leading a team of people. This notion we have to be at the top to be leaders is becoming out of date. In fact, forward-thinking organisations are now structuring themselves without layers and hierarchy for exactly this reason. There's no boss in the corner office; leaders naturally evolve as groups of self-managing teams come together to work on different projects.

Look at your current role and you'll probably find elements of leadership – meetings you might have to chair, projects you're in charge of, a new starter you mentor, colleagues you support and advise. We are often using leadership skills every day, regardless of our job titles, just in terms of how we lead and manage ourselves in daily life, but we tend not to see this unless it comes with a formal 'manager' title.

When we're faced with applying for a new job or a promotion, though, we look at our CVs and current job titles and the same fear arises: 'I don't think I can do that job. I'm underqualified.' Even if we have most of the skills required, we tend to lean towards modesty and underestimate our achievements and capabilities. We can be terrified we might not do a good job and fail or we're just simply not as good as this job will need us to be. We tend to think, 'Oh, I haven't done that before,' rather than, 'I could probably learn that.'

I remember having these fears and reservations when I applied for a job I eventually excelled in and outgrew in the first year. When I got an interview and then ultimately the offer, I was plagued with the thought, 'They will find out I'm not capable, I'm not as good as they think I am, and I think this job might be too big for me.' I even remember having to google the definition of *implementing strategy* and *organisational development*.

The job description made it sound so much harder than it was in practice. I soon realised *implementing strategy* in layman's terms was making stuff happen and bringing plans into action, and this was my speciality. It dawned on me from this experience it's not that we can't do the jobs or haven't had the experience. So often we know this stuff – it's just by another name. We have the experience but often in different areas of life or known by different words. Knowing our transferable skills is key, and there are so many roles these can be relevant in.

This is one of the main things that can hold us back in our careers – doubting our abilities but also feeling we need to have 100% of the job description done with years of experience. We feel we need to be 100% perfect before promotion, when really 60% will do if we also possess transferable skills and an enthusiasm to learn.

It's common for there to be a gender difference in this space too. The research tells us women are more likely to doubt themselves and underestimate their suitability for the role in question. If this resonates for you, some of these top tips for progressing your career might be useful.

- Know yourself, and know what you want
- Empower yourself – own it
- Align to your values
- Have an open mind
- Learn and reflect
- Take credit for your work
- Take your opportunities – and deliver
- Be resilient
- Trust your intuition
- Find a mentor
- Leverage your strengths

- Set goals
- Face your fears and get out of your comfort zone

Your employment brand

There's the traditional way to apply for jobs, via jobs boards and application processes or recruitment agents, but there's also another effective method that's particularly prevalent among small populations. This is true for New Zealand and also niche industries where the degrees of separation seem smaller.

Even in larger populations, never underestimate the power of your network. Most companies rely on a fair selection process, but first we have to get into that process and this is where who you know can be an advantage. Sometimes getting a foot in the door for consideration in the first place can be as much about who you know as what you know.

If your brand is a credible one, this is a powerful lever to pull. We know the impact this has because of the way we purchase. If we know the people selling the product or the brand name on it is credible, we're more likely to buy it. Even more so if we've had a word-of-mouth recommendation about that product from someone we trust. Now image this for your career prospects.

Someone who's worked with you in the past recommends you to your new boss. The person interviewing you happened to see you speak at a conference or has seen articles you post about your field of expertise on LinkedIn. Already you have the edge over a total stranger (even a very qualified one).

It's about trust, and it's the foundation of relationship building and key to being seen as credible. It's also less of a risk for the person making the appointment. The more I know about you and your expertise, even from others (as long as I trust them), the more likely I am to hire you. All this happens before you've had one day on the job to prove you're capable.

It's why it's important when we do leave a business we do so on goods terms, even if it's tempting to take a parting shot. Remember your brand and how word travels across our towns, cities and industries.

In these days of LinkedIn and social media, our brand is out there more than ever and our network is often larger too. See who you know that works with a company you're keen to get into or find influential people you can follow and engage with across LinkedIn. Showing up and showing your expertise is now far easier than impressing the boss with your delivery on the job. There may be professional associations, networking events, conferences and meet-ups. These all provide opportunities to expand your network and expose your brand.

Decisions made about our career progression generally happen when we're not in the room. That's why it's important to have brand champions or at least know your brand and how to demonstrate it. It's an exercise I often do in my leadership development programmes.

So, what's your brand? Generally it's not something we may have thought about, but it'll be there nonetheless. It's something that emerges over time based on how we show up, interact with others and deliver. Let me ask you: what are you known for? If you left tomorrow, what would your boss or peers miss most? What do people say about you when you're not in the room?

It might be you're the go-to person on a certain topic. It might be your attention to detail, your trusting guidance or your problem-solving skills. It might be your ability to relate to others or navigate a conflict or your excellent customer service.

Whilst we'll have a brand that has been developed over time by people's experience of us, we also get a chance to think now about the kind of brand we'd like to create and how we get known for that.

Think of a pair of shoes. They're uncomfortable and break within a few weeks – what do you think about the brand now? Regardless of what it says above the shop door, think about what you'll tell your friends about those shoes if anyone asks if you'd recommend that brand? Equally, the reverse of that is true, which is why some of us spend years buying the same style of shoes.

It goes without saying one of the foundations of a good brand is doing what we say we will, delivering on expectations and not letting people down. Integrity is the foundation of trust and imperative where brand is concerned.

Our brand is what people know us for – our reputation. It's how we demonstrate our credibility and be known for who we are and what we stand for. How do you ensure you're clear about your brand and known for this? When building your brand goals, think about the value you bring to the table.

1. What are your natural strengths?
2. What do you do extremely well?
3. What do people acknowledge you for?
4. How do you add value at work?

Now write down three words that describe you, what these words mean to you and what they look like in action. I've included an example.

Words that describe you	What do they mean to you?	What action demonstrates this?
Compassionate	*I care about others*	*I take time to lend my coaching skills over coffee*
1.		
2.		
3.		

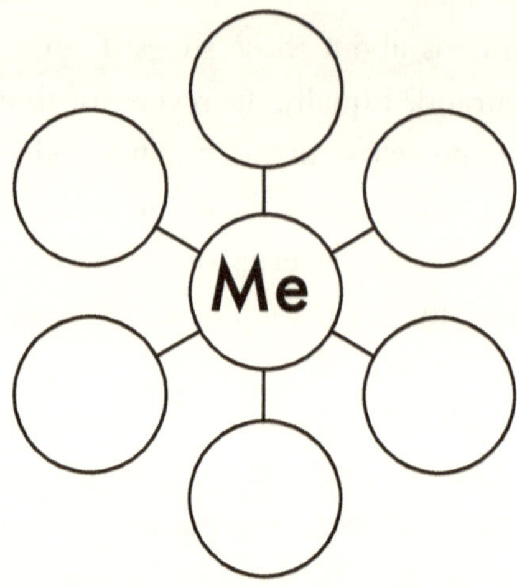

Now do the same for three words others use to describe you (go ahead and ask them for an accurate answer).

Words that describe you	What do they mean to you?	What action demonstrates this?
1.		
2.		
3.		

Is there a match or some recurring themes? Look back on some of your strengths and values exercises for some inspiration here too, as there's likely to be crossover.

Next, put that into a statement. Now, this is something that might make its way on to our CV or LinkedIn profile, but we also have to ensure we're backing it up in action. Why is this powerful? What's the question we get asked the most when we meet someone new? 'What do you do?'

Think of this in the context of applying for jobs or career progression. It's often called an elevator pitch. If you got into the elevator with the CEO of the company you'd always wanted to work for and they asked you, 'What do you do?' you'd have until the lift got to the floor to respond in a way that made them remember you (positively)!

Now, quite often we answer with the facts – 'I'm an accounts assistant at Barnardos,' for example. Whilst this may be true, it doesn't tell me anything about who you are, why you do that or your point of difference – what makes you special?

Now, if you were to respond with, 'My attention to detail and knowledge of fundraising help improve the lives of children across the country,' much more 'wow' and I get a sense of who you are and why you do what you do. I also know what you're good at or known for. More than this, though, it makes me want to ask you more and engage in conversation; it sounds interesting.

Both statements are true, but can you see how much more impactful the latter is? Now try the same for your job. What if my job is quite boring, though, or I don't work for a charity changing the world? Maybe you're a call centre team leader – 'I use my mentoring skills to support and develop the next generation of communication experts.'

So now we've got our brand clear, how do we get people to know about it? Some of this will just be by simply showing up and doing our thing – bringing this stuff to life in the way we work every day and how we show up with others. There are ways we can amplify this, though, and we've talked about the power of networks, especially in today's online world.

Identify the opportunities that exist for you. People you want to get to know, ways you can broaden your network, groups you can be part of or events you could attend.

Making a stakeholder map can be useful in this instance. You put yourself in the middle and then draw lines to all the people who currently know you or could. This will be your boss, peers, colleagues. Those in your network, industry, past colleagues. Include on this map those you've yet to make contact with but you'd like to know your brand – the CEO of the company you've always wanted to work for, as an example, or the leader of the team you've been vying for promotion into.

Once you've got this list, it becomes much easier to see the opportunities for expanding your network and elevating your brand and therefore your impact.

I worked with a client who volunteered to be on the wellness committee of her organisation because she knew it was a way of demonstrating her brand to her potential new boss (the team she'd always wanted to be part of) who was also on the committee. This is just one example, but you'll find your own.

We've talked about ikigai and the importance of purpose, and this comes in here too. People remember your why; they don't necessarily buy what you do but *why* you do it, and this becomes part of your brand.

The bottom line is if we know our brand and it's genuine, people will notice. It's how we connect and build trust. It's being authentic, and this is at the heart of our integrity. People want to know the person they're connecting with is genuine, and if they think we're trying to fake it or not showing up as our true selves, we'll struggle to trust them. This is why connecting to your brand and purpose is so key.

'The biggest turning point was finding my why'
Tabitha Arthur is a photographer who owns her own portrait photography business. Previously, she was a graphic designer.
When I was a graphic designer, I always enjoyed talking with clients to find out what drove them and what their passions were, but I hated being left behind a soulless computer screen alone. I sometimes felt lost, like there was no point to

the work I was doing, as I limped to the finish line on each project. I wrestled internally with working with clients on campaigns that conflicted with my values, such as promoting meat (I'm a vegetarian). This, along with long hours and a serious dose of imposter syndrome, eventually impacted my health to the point of hospitalisation.

I knew I had to change what I was doing, but I didn't know what else I could do. I sought the support of a counsellor, who helped me start to connect the dots in my life. I left my workplace and did some soul-searching whilst freelancing in the arts, an industry that is a passion of mine. I started mentoring young graphic designers and began to get my mojo back when I saw how I could have a positive impact on others.

The biggest turning point was finding my why – I didn't even know that was a thing! It was when I was creating some of my own marketing material for my arts projects I became aware I could affect the way people felt about themselves through taking their photos. It gave me a growing sense of purpose outside myself, and I was working from a place of joy.

I strove to become better at taking photographs. I began educating myself through online courses, and I eventually enrolled in a coaching programme with a portrait photographer that focused on how people feel about themselves and how we bring this to the client experience as well as taking great photos. I learned about business, money value, self-belief and mindset, and I immersed myself in this development. The best part was the more I learned and developed myself, the more my confidence and clarity grew. I'm in control of what I do with my own business, I have a strong sense of purpose, and I get to make an impact and a positive difference for the clients I work with, which has a ripple effect out into the world. I've never got up so early. My work fuels me with energy and purpose, and I feel I am finally thriving.

CVs and interviews

So, once we know all this and have our brand front and centre, how do we prepare for our dream job? Being in HR was a privileged role in this space. Having been on many recruitment panels over the years and privy to many hiring decisions, seen thousands of CVs and the best and worst of interview performance, I love sharing this with others. It's a glimpse at being on the other side of the table, and it can help us put our best foot forward.

Preparation is the key; knowing the market and the organisation you're applying to as well as knowing your point of difference and why they should hire you are all key points to consider. Do your homework, talk to people you know who've worked there in the past, see if you know anyone who works there now. What's the culture like? What do they look for in an employee? Is it a good fit for you? Why?

Your CV will get you a foot in the door, but if it's too long, people won't read it. These days, hiring managers get hundreds of CVs. How does yours stand out, and why will I put it in the yes pile? At best, most skim-read until the interview stage, so make sure when they skim your CV, the most important, relevant information is what they see. Add to this the use of automated systems and it's also pleasing the algorithms we've got to consider now!

It needs to be to the point and capture the best bits first to leave a good impression and secure the interview. But what should you include on your CV?

Where work experience is concerned, I always suggest only

include it if it's relevant (would the hiring manager want to know this, will this get me extra points?). Order the most recent first, as people want to know where you're at now, not the job you had 10 years ago, before you became qualified to apply for this one.

Key achievements can be preferable in place of duties. Often duties are implied once you state your job title, so using this space to talk about your key achievements in that role can set you apart.

Similarly, a brief paragraph at the top summarising your skills and expertise can be helpful in terms of drawing the attention of the reader in. Bullet lists of your top skills and experience are clear and concise (as long as they're not too long).

Things like hobbies, date of birth and photos – again, all irrelevant, unless you think it'll give you the edge or is necessary for the role. For example, an application to a modelling agency may be best with a photo, but otherwise it's not necessary.

References can always be available on request at this point in the process, and this takes up less room on your CV as well as avoiding any premature phone calls to your current boss before you've told them you're applying for another job!

Think outside of the box, too; it's not just about your work experience. If you've been the chair of a community group or project managed your new build – all transferable skills that may help you in your next role, so think broadly. Think of experience you've gained in voluntary roles and community groups; perhaps you're captain of your sports team, maybe you lead certain projects at work or chair the team meetings, perhaps you mentor new graduates. There will be many experiences you've had that demonstrate leadership and other skills and may be relevant for this role.

Beyond this, we should be able to request a copy of the job description and person specification. This will give us a clue to what's important and what kind of questions they're likely to ask at interview. I spend time going through these with my coaching clients, highlighting key points. If the job description talks of project management, managing conflict and navigating change, you can bet these will come up as questions, so be prepared by being able to talk through examples of how you've demonstrated this in your previous roles.

It's not just about ticking boxes with your skills these days. Just because you've been a project manager for 10 years doesn't mean you'll tick the boxes on the interviewer's form. What sets you apart from other project managers with 10 years' experience?

Most businesses use competency-based interview questions and situational techniques. What this means is they'll be asking you to demonstrate a particular competency (for example, project management) using an example. So you talk through a time you've managed a particular project through to completion. What was it, what did you do, what went well, what were the challenges, how did you overcome them?

Using this technique allows interviewers to separate different kinds of project managers and get an insight into their approach and strengths. Sometimes, depending on the business, they're also looking for you to mention certain things they feel are important, like bringing others along on the journey or stakeholder management, for example.

Preparation is key. Have certain examples you can talk through for the competencies likely to come up (based on the job description they provide). My advice is to practise this like a script so you can easily articulate it when asked. You'll also want some key points prepared that you feel are important and want to remember to cover. For example, if you've won an award for your work recently or worked for a competitor in the past and bring some inside knowledge, make sure you mention that.

Beyond this, it's just as much about remaining calm and composed. This helps enormously. I don't know anyone who enjoys being interviewed, and it can bring about nerves in the best of us.

With all that considered, you put your best foot forward and get offered a new job or a promotion. What about negotiations and getting paid the right amount for this job? How do we even know what that is?

'Look at the companies you admire and what you're passionate about'

Samantha Gadd is the CEO of Humankind, formerly HR Shop.

At Humankind, we are all about helping people love what they do, which has evolved now to leading humanity at work. Loving our work is all about our ability to make a difference and being able to celebrate our success and the success of our clients.

I was a life coach before I started this business, and some of my most satisfying days at work were coaching people to help them to love what they do. I have a deep belief that we need to love what we do, because we spend so much time at work.

I decided very early on I wanted to run my own business. I wanted to be in control of my own destiny, but it's come with a lot of hard work – probably harder than I've ever worked. Working long hours feels less like hard work when you love it, though.

I love growing something and knowing it's of value; I love creating brands, building stuff and creating something from nothing. The opportunity to do that and bring things to life is really cool.

Individuals should know what success looks like for themselves on a daily basis without external validation; this helps job satisfaction. It's a leader's role to help people understand this through role clarity, connection to strategy and clear measures.

My knowledge from our employee-experience work tells me leadership is everything; it's the biggest lever organisations can pull. If you're working for someone you trust and believe in, someone who cares about you, that makes a huge difference. If you don't like your job, go and find a great leader; it almost doesn't matter what job you're doing. People join companies but leave bosses. If you don't have a great leader, find that somewhere else, look for leadership in other areas, get a great mentor instead.

People generally choose their job because of the opportunity, career progression, more money, sometimes it's an industry they want to succeed in. I often encourage people rather than looking via listings based on job title and career progression to look at what companies you want to work for and how your skills can add value to these businesses. Rather than looking at SEEK, look at the companies you admire and what you're passionate about and approach it from this perspective.

I've hired people based on fit rather than skills, and they've progressed within the business even in roles they've not done before. If someone shows a particular passion, interest and knowledge about my business, it puts them streets ahead of anyone else in that group. Even if someone was super qualified, I'd think twice about employing them if they didn't show an interest in the work we do.

Negotiating salary

We women, in particular, tend to undervalue ourselves and therefore underprice our services, rather than thinking, 'What is my work worth? What will people pay?' It's a similar story when negotiating salary increases or new job packages. We settle for less.

I remember when I left the United Kingdom to move to New Zealand, I was involved in recruiting my replacement. We had a great candidate, he was an ideal fit, but he was asking way more than the budget. I spoke to the managing director, and we agreed time was short and he was ideal, so let's just make him the offer.

It was a full £20,000 a year more than I was on, and I'm sure I could have asked for that to stay, had I not been emigrating, but I never would.

The chances are, if I did, I'd have been told that kind of pay hike is unreasonable and would have been offered something in between. That experience was a reminder of value and price for me. What's the job worth, what would the company pay, rather than what do I need to live off, what am I on now, and what would be a reasonable request in my undervalued mind?

My advice is to always ask for more than you think you want. The worst that can happen is it's turned down and you get what you wanted anyway. But make sure your request is reasonable and in line with market rates. It's important, therefore, to do your homework, so you know what the salary range of the job is (i.e., the lowest and highest amounts they'd be willing to pay). Use online salary information to understand what the job is worth in the market, remembering to take into account impacts such as location, industry and experience, which often make a difference to salary weighting.

There's also much more to a job than salary, and research tells us it's not always the biggest motivating factor in our jobs. Asking for more annual leave, flexible working or other benefits such as healthcare and access to the company bonus scheme, if applicable to the role, can all be good ways of negotiating outside of base salary.

It can be something we struggle with, though. The art of negotiating or asking for more. What if they give it to someone else? What if they think I'm pushy? Will I have to work twice as hard to earn it if I ask for more? These are all questions that commonly arise. We're not taught to talk about money, and in past generations, we've been taught to just be grateful we've got a job, so we say yes to the first offer without thinking about whether it's got the right price tag attached to it.

When we say right price tag, we of course mean in line with the market and your skills and experience for the business in question and the location the business is in. There are so many variables, but the one we most often consider is the one that shouldn't come into it: what's my current salary? Is a 10% increase too much? What do I need to live off? Whilst these questions might seem logical when we're changing jobs, they shouldn't impact the salary on the paperwork. That should be about the role, not the individual's circumstances.

If I'm making a career change, a sideways move, working for a competitor or relocating, my current salary will not be comparable. Similarly, if I've just spent four years out of the workforce bringing up children, my current salary with bear no relation to the current market.

The best time to ask for a pay rise is always before we start a job; our biggest pay rise will generally come when we change jobs. Negotiating a job offer leaves more bargaining room than annual increments once employed, which are often part of a pre-agreed scale or related to business performance or a small budget that's spread across the entire company.

But how often are we so pleased to get the job, to be the preferred candidate, we forget to ask? How often have you just said 'yes' – without even asking about salary?

It's not uncommon for people I work with to negotiate a 10–20% higher salary with their new job offers. It's almost impossible to get this kind of raise as an annual increment, no matter how well we're performing, because of salary review budgets, policies and the fact it's every employee in the business asking at this time of year, not just you!

It's easy to naively assume we'll be paid what the job is worth, the market rate, but sadly experience proves if we don't ask, we often don't get, no matter how valuable we are.

How often do we assume after working hard for a year and earning the company a lot of money, we'll be rewarded accordingly and our effort will not go unnoticed?

It's this and the fact most of us feel uncomfortable asking that stop us being paid what we deserve. We may have been brought up not to talk about money: 'It's rude to ask, be thankful you've got a job, don't come across as too pushy.' All these things play into our fears about what is simply asking the question.

But it's easier said than done. Although in theory asking seems straightforward, it makes most people I know (especially women) feel uncomfortable, and we worry how we'll be judged.

I find it's often better if this is done by phone or email at offer stage, as there's something less confronting about talking this stuff through when it's not face to face as part of an interview process, which is already uncomfortable enough. It also allows you to have a script in front of you and deal with the feelings that ultimately come up when we discuss something we've been conditioned not to mention.

Here are a few more tips to make it easier and to know when and how to ask.

1. Do your research

Be informed; know the market rate and where you fit into it. Take into account the industry you work in, the location you work in, the availability in your market – are people like you in short supply? Much of this information is available online through jobs boards and recruitment agency websites.

2. Know your worth

Ask for a range/band before the interview so you know the minimum and maximum they'd pay someone for the role, and pitch yourself within that range based on your skills and experience and your point of difference. For example, are you coming from a competitor? Do you bring a lot of experience or a unique skill?

Remember your current salary shouldn't come into it. If you're at an interview and they ask, 'What's your current salary?' your response can still be, 'My *expected* salary for this role is between x and y.'

As you've done your market research and know the range or band for the role, you can pitch yourself within that. There are so many reasons why our current salary shouldn't come into this conversation, unless it's an internal promotion, and of course we've no way of avoiding that.

3. Think beyond base salary

There's more to it than money – and that means more options for negotiation. An extra week's leave, health benefits, gym membership, bonus schemes, flexible working. It all contributes to our package, and often some of this is worth more to us than money.

4. Don't give up too soon

Even after the interview, if a job offer is made, it's still not too late to negotiate salary. If the job offer comes to you with a figure on it, you can always ask for more. Do your homework and go back with a valid reason, saying, 'I'm excited about the opportunity. A salary of x is more in line with my expectations for this role/my skills and experience etc.'

5. Just ask the question

The worst they can say is no, and then you can accept the job on the current terms (if you're happy to).

Chapter 8

Work–life balance and high performance

WE'VE LANDED OUR dream job, or maybe we've been able to make some changes to our existing job to find the joy and learn to love our Mondays. Either way, one of the key markers of success is our ability to perform well and how sustainable we are. In this chapter, we'll learn how to build resilience and manage our workload. This includes understanding the difference between busy and productive as well as the impacts of perfectionism and a high-achiever drive that can so often lead to burnout. We'll also look at the keys to high performance and how to master our mindset for success. Before we go there, though, we first need to understand the importance of wellness to sustain our energy and master the art of work–life balance.

Workplace wellness and work–life balance

Many workers spend upwards of 40 hours per week on the job, and a large number go as far as to regularly log in after hours and on weekends to get the job done. Fear of falling behind is leading to 50% of US employees' forfeiting their paid vacation, with 10% taking no vacation days at all, according to a study by recruitment website Glassdoor.

For so long, we've talked about this quest for work–life balance, and yet it's seemed elusive for many. I even went to the great lengths of becoming my own boss to escape the nine-to-five, only to then work even more hours setting up my own business! It's led me to the conclusion there is no work–life balance. It's all life, and it should all balance, which includes a bit of work within that life.

As flexible working becomes more common, we are seeing less commuting and traditional office hours. We can come in late if we've got medical appointments or school drop-offs and leave early if we're logging on that night from home to finish off. We can nip out for yoga over lunchtime when we're working from home or put a load of washing on and meet a friend for coffee. This is balance, and it happens whilst we work.

There's a direct correlation between workplace satisfaction and our health and happiness. In 2018, NZ Stats reported not being happy at work impacted on our health and happiness in life. Only 16% of people who were satisfied with their job reported having poor mental wellbeing. This increased to 43% of those who were unsatisfied with their job. Furthermore, those who were dissatisfied with their jobs were more likely to have felt lonely in the last four weeks.

Workplace wellness has become big business, and most organisations are well aware of the benefits. Employees who are not well don't deliver optimal performance; it's that simple. As much as wellness initiatives at work can help, the free fruit, lunchtime yoga classes and gym memberships will only go so far. Our health is our responsibility, and we must be accountable for our wellness. For the benefit of our life, not just our work.

I learned this the hard way. I worked long hours – if I wasn't in meetings, I was in the car, driving. I'd grab fast food because it was quick and I could eat on the run. After getting in late, I was so exhausted exercise was the last thing I felt like doing, so I'd crash on the sofa and then get my laptop out to catch up on emails.

I spent my weekends sleeping in and catching up on all the housework I'd let slide during the week, and I was usually sick during my vacations as my body struggled to cope with the constant demands. I knew it wasn't healthy but wasn't sure how to change it, how to find balance. When I looked around, I realised everyone else seemed to be doing the same.

Eventually, I hit a wall and burned out. This ultimately led to a fork in the road where everything changed. Reflecting on this experience helped me develop the advice I give to others now. Here are my tips for thriving at work (even if you're not in a job you love).

1. Adopt a healthy routine

I found adopting a healthy routine made things easier. I get up early so I can meditate and do a bit of yoga. This sets me up for the day and makes me feel good before I even get to work. Getting up early means I have time for breakfast and to walk to my office. It's a challenge at first, and the snooze button is always tempting, but once we feel the benefits, it's a no-brainer. And after a few weeks of doing this, it becomes a habit. This can be a challenge if you've been up since 3am or have three kids to look after, but we'll talk more about routines and finding space for self-care shortly.

2. Take care of your body

Work can be stressful, which is why paying attention to the basics of good health and prioritising this makes our workdays better. What we eat, how much water we drink, how much we move, the lighting, the ventilation, how we sit – it all adds up. It may seem simple, but it's also important.

The meals we choose fuel us throughout the day; we know we can feel lethargic and short of energy if we're not eating right. We are what we eat, so it's critical we're putting the right things in to help us thrive both at work and at home. It has a direct impact on our mood, how we concentrate and, therefore, how much better we're likely to deal with stress and demanding colleagues.

Exercise is also key, especially for those of us who are deskbound. I ensure I get up and move around regularly, either to get water, to talk to a colleague or when I'm on the phone. I also make sure I get outside every lunchtime for a walk and some fresh air and head to the gym some evenings to counteract all the sitting my job requires.

3. Make it a priority to have fun with co-workers

Human beings are social animals, and our colleagues can be the source of great company. Taking time out to ask people how they're doing, chatting about plans for the weekend or doing the quiz over morning tea is a pleasant addition to the workday.

There are many ways to bond with your colleagues: Friday night drinks after closing, lunchtime walking groups, social sports teams, quiz nights and office morning teas. It's a great way of getting to know your colleagues better, outside of the formalities of work agendas.

4. Treat yourself

Every week I treat myself to dinner at my favourite café, or takeout if I'm tired. It's usually on a Friday, and I often spend the week looking forward to this. I also have a massage once a month, partly to offset sitting at a computer but also to treat myself and show my body some love. It's the little things I look forward to, which my wages allow me to buy, which make working more worthwhile.

5. Spend time in nature

This one makes a big difference, particularly if we live and work in cities and may be confined inside without natural light or ventilation. Get out during lunchtime for a walk in the park, or spend the weekend camping at the beach or in a cabin in the woods. Whatever it is, make sure you get some time in nature. It helps us unwind, relax and reconnect, not just to the natural world around us but also to ourselves. Science is proving nature really does have healing powers, and I know it's a vital part of helping me thrive at work.

6. Strive for balance

I learned the hard way, and now work–life balance is one of my top priorities. I see many people who seem defined by their jobs; this is their lives and who they are, and this mantra often takes over their lives.

If we spend all our hours at work, there are areas of our life we're neglecting – perhaps time with loved ones, time to ourselves or social events or hobbies. Work–life balance is so important. After all, one of the reasons we go to work is so we can afford to have a life!

7. Do what you love

They say if you love what you do, you'll be successful. While not all of us have the jobs we've dreamed of since we were young, we can often find things within our jobs we enjoy – dealing with people, training others, designing posters, solving problems or organising events.

When the hard days at work come, I put them into perspective and ensure I find a positive. I also make sure I find time to do something I love, whether it's writing, walking outside in nature or having lunch with friends.

8. Never forget your 'why'

Probably the most important thing is not to lose sight of our reasons for going to work. Yes, we need to earn money, and preferably we do this doing something we love. But sometimes we have to do X in order to get to Y. Remember your 'why'. This could be your kids' education, that trip of a lifetime, your first home or a medical treatment for a family member.

Put a photo on your desk that'll remind you every day what you're working for. It's not the boss who doesn't know your name or the company that cares more about its bottom line. It's for your hopes and dreams and all the things you do each month with the wages you're lucky to earn.

We spend so much time at work, it makes sense we make it as happy as it can be. It doesn't have to be detrimental to our health. This can be as much about our attitude towards busyness and self-care as the workplace itself. By mastering the art of balance, we can thrive at work.

> **'I've got a happy balance now'**
> *Nadine works in accounting and contract management for a recruitment company.*
> I picked accounting at school because I was good at it, but I didn't know if it would turn into my career. I met my current boss through the local Plunket group, and I've been there for 15 years now. It's a part-time role, so it fits well around my kids and life.
> My hours can be flexible, and I feel like I add value at work. I can be helping a contractor at 10.30pm with their tax, but I can also take the morning off to do some voluntary work.
> I volunteer doing grants at my children's colleges to fund sporting equipment and trips. My work are very supportive

of allowing me time to do this. It's important to me to give back.

I've had other accounting jobs during this time, but these jobs haven't been the same. It's the company culture. They care about their clients and each other, and we all pull together to get through. In previous jobs, I experienced office politics, and with kids, I didn't have the energy for that. As I get older, office politics interest me less, and I really appreciate the honesty of where I work now.

I enjoy empowering people to make decisions with my accounting knowledge. I also tend to get involved in quite a few financial decisions in this position. Whether it's buying a new company or something else, I get to be involved. I've learned a lot from my previous managers: how they deal with people and the culture they create, and the way they've helped me, appreciated me and developed my skills.

I want my children to know Mum was there and that I'm a good person to deal with. I used to feel like I should do more work and contribute more to our income, but working full time, I missed out on too much and the family was suffering because of that, so I've got a happy balance now.

High performance and resilience

Now we've got the job we love, we want to make sure we can keep it. We want to flourish in that job. Particularly if it's our own business, our success (and salary) is determined by our own personal performance.

Once we know what we want to do and have prepared to make the move, we then need to ensure sustainability and success. We want to deliver and maintain high performance. This, of course, also helps our continuing brand, our health and our happiness.

The terms 'high performance' and 'delivering results' are often used in business, but what does it really mean to exceed expectations, and how do we ensure our performance is exceptional?

Wellness and balance help us perform well. They also help build resilience, which in turn helps us navigate change and bounce back from setbacks. These are often the things we sacrifice, though, in the name of hard work and high performance. How do we navigate this conflict, and what are the other factors to consider where high performance is concerned?

We all want to perform well in our jobs, to exceed expectations and be rewarded. This can often be what drives us to work too hard. Before we look at workload and productivity, we need to first understand what high performance is and why it's important, then we'll discover how to hit that mark without going too far and leaving the tank empty.

It makes sense that when we hit the mark of high performance we're more likely to progress in our career and obtain promotions, but it's a careful balance. One that can often end in busyness, perfectionism and workload overwhelm, so let's explore it further here.

Aside from our knowledge and skill set, and the experience we bring to our job (which for the purpose of this section I'm going to assume is a given), what else makes up high performance?

- Good health – energy and resilience
- Good habits and routine
- Leveraging strengths
- Goals and growth
- Learning and reflection (self-awareness)
- Mindset
- Support (including delegation)

Resilience and self-care

Resilience is our ability to bounce back from tough times. Resilient people can motivate themselves in the face of setbacks; they are optimistic; they learn from their mistakes, solve problems and look for solutions. They have self-control and are not afraid to seek assistance from others.

Things don't always go to plan; we have to deal with challenging situations or people. Resilient people perform better and are healthier and happier.

If you've heard me talk about this, you'll know I'm an advocate for this being a constant focus, not just when we need it. It's too late at that point. I liken it to a bank account we pay into over time, so we can withdraw funds when we need them, when the tough times hit.

It's easy to be happy when everything is going well, but we know that's not always the case, and that's why we should be building our resilience and looking after ourselves. Because tough times come to us all at some point. Whilst we can't always control the things that happen to us, we do control how we react to them, and a massive determining factor in this space is our resilience.

The uncertainty and business pivoting that's resulted since Covid-19 has been a test in this space, as we've all struggled to change our jobs, working patterns and workload, all amid the economic uncertainty and lack of job security a global pandemic brings.

A tree grows its roots when the weather is fine so when the storms come, it stays standing strong. If we wait until we need resilience to start building it, we'll find we'll be trying to grow roots in the midst of a storm.

Buddhists have a great analogy for this, which sums up perfectly how attitude and mindset impact our resilience. It's called the second arrow analogy. If we're walking through the forest and we get hit by an arrow, we have a problem, and it causes us pain. Our reaction to this problem is like being hit by a second arrow in the same place. Now we have two problems and double the pain, the difference being the second arrow we shot ourself.

It's not about what happens to us but how we react to it. The second arrow represents our reaction, getting upset and angry about the initial problem. For example, the car may have broken down, and we are inconvenienced. That is our first arrow and the resulting pain. If we choose to get angry and upset about this, our reaction is the equivalent of shooting the second arrow. It will double our pain but do little to resolve the first problem, and we did it to ourselves.

We spend a lot of our time trying to avoid the bad things in life while simultaneously chasing after the good. We cling on when we get something good, hoping it'll never leave, yet in reality both good and bad will always come and go.

Regardless of who we work for and what job we have, we will come across people who frustrate us, people who underperform and people who think and act differently to us. We'll also likely be involved in restructures or even redundancies and have to leave a job or adapt to a change not of our own choice.

One of the tools I often use in my workshops is Stephen Covey's circle of influence. It really helps cut through the worries to empower us to take action and take control over the things we can influence.

We all have a wide range of concerns in our life. Things we care about that affect us but we have little or no control over.

Some of this we can influence, some of it we can't. We have a choice about which we choose to spend our time and energy focusing on. If we focus on all of our concerns and worries, we might find they get bigger with the attention we give them, but we'll also not be able to take any significant action, we'll get depressed and nothing much will change. It leads to blame and feelings of victimisation.

Things like this belong in the outer circle and are things that affect us but we have no control over, like the stock market, war, pandemics, government policy, or traffic jams. Spending our time and energy worrying about these things we can do nothing about doesn't change them and can make us feel reactive, like a victim, and lead to blame and a feeling of helplessness.

When we focus on the things we can influence – the inner circle – we become more proactive. Things we can control are inside our circle of influence, and focusing on this inner circle means the efforts make a more positive difference in relationships and results.

This can be as simple as our reaction to something or aspects of huge problems we can exert some influence over. It doesn't mean direct control; for example, we might not be able to stop climate change, but we can focus on our own behaviour and what we do around our home to help contribute in this space.

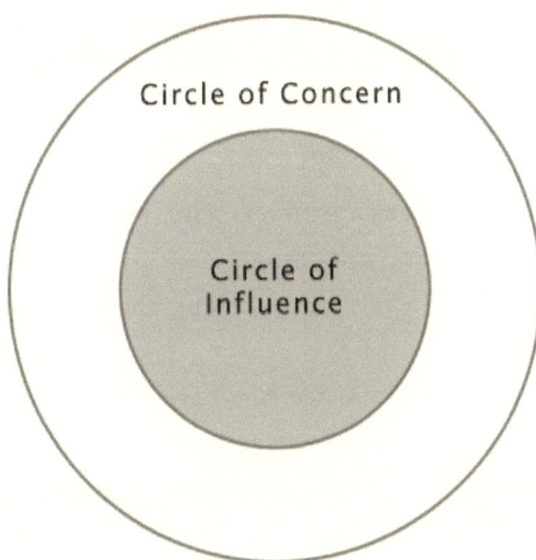

When we focus our energy here, it enlarges the inner circle and therefore our influence. It's liberating to know we can make a difference and control even small aspects of our concerns when they are within our circle of influence.

If the business we work for is closing and we're being made redundant, there's nothing we can do about that; it sits in the outer circle. However, the things that sit in the inner circle might be updating our CV, seeking outplacement support or talking to a friend who said last week their brother might be looking for new staff.

We want our focus to be on those things we can control or influence and away from the things we have no control over. Don't waste energy on things you can't do anything about.

As the Dalai Lama put it, 'If there is a solution to the problem, then great, we don't need to worry. If there isn't a solution to the problem, then there's no point worrying about it.'

Take a look at the circle diagram and consider some of your own concerns.

- Which circle are you spending most of your time and energy in?

- What are some of your current concerns, and which circle do they fall in? Which ones fall in the inner circle, and what can you do about them?

It can even be done as a team exercise. Put a larger copy of this diagram on the wall and encourage team members to add Post-it Notes of concerns in each circle, asking the question each time, 'What can we do about this?'

So what other ways can we build resilience? We'll talk about self-care next and how this impacts our resilience, as well as mindset, which plays a massive role. Before that, here are some top tips to help boost the positive and build your resilience.

- Exercise
- Meditation
- Spending time with good friends
- Connecting with nature

- Giving yourself permission to play
- Practising acts of kindness
- Counting your blessings each day
- Savouring goodness
- Using your strengths in a new way
- Injecting joy into your day (like your favourite song)
- Reframing negative events in a positive way

Are you busy or productive?

The majority of people I speak to say they don't have time, and that's the whole problem. The fact we are too busy to take time out to relax is the precise reason it's so important we do. In a world that encourages noise and busyness, we find it so hard to be quiet and still, yet it is a necessary part of good health and resilience building.

Our attachment to busy has meant we've deprioritised downtime and pauses from our lives, because these are seen as a waste of time when we could be doing something 'productive'. By trying to maximise every second of every day, we've removed all the opportunities to rest and recharge and have no space left in our lives.

Self-care is often viewed as a nice-to-have, something to do when we get a spare few minutes or when the to-do list is done. It's something we leave until we've got time and don't prioritise when we're busy. The irony is this is the time we probably need it most.

We worry it might be seen as selfish, lazy or unproductive to take some downtime. Yet it's critical in helping us build resilience and perform at our peak.

If you take time out for yourself, it's not only you that benefits. Imagine what a better partner, parent and worker you'd be if you weren't stressed and tired, how much more you could give others and how much better your relationships would be. Taking time out for yourself is anything but selfish; everyone benefits from a better, more refreshed you.

The bottom line is the more we do in a day, the less we'll do well, because it's coupled with a sense of overwhelm and exhaustion and, as a result, we can't be at our best. The problem stems from this attachment we have to busy, the way it's been made fashionable and attached to success, and also from the fact we believe we're being productive.

Ask anyone at work how their day is going, and most of the time they'll respond with, 'Busy,' even if they're not actually that busy. It's a word that implies successful, valuable, performing, and it's sought after at work. It shows people you're productive and effective at your job. Or does it?

In a world where burnout and overwhelm are so common, being busy may not be the gold star we've been led to believe. Being busy does not mean we're productive or effective; in fact, it could mean the opposite.

Let's explore the difference between busy and productive. In this space, I believe less is sometimes more, and it's a concept I refer to as slowing down to speed up.

I know that sounds counterintuitive in a world where we're taught we should be doing more things in less time and multitasking is a must. But we know the more we juggle, the more likely it is we make mistakes. We also know the more we have on our plate, the greater the sense of overwhelm, the less healthy we feel and the more tired we get – none of this is a recipe for high performance.

We perform best when we're rested, refreshed and not stressed. When we can focus on the task at hand, without interruption, and complete it using our skills.

We need to start seeing self-care and time out as a must-have, a priority, not a nice-to-have, luxury item reserved for when we've got time, when the to-do list is complete (because it never is). If we take time out, feel rested and refreshed, get a good night's sleep, take the time to exercise and eat right, we can perform better. This means things don't take as long, we've got more energy, we can make decisions and solve problems quicker and generally we get it done right the first time.

If we slow down by taking small pauses in our day to recharge and press reset, we find we're more effective when we return to our day. If we are clear-headed and well-rested, we function better; we get things done more quickly, navigate setbacks with ease and have more space to innovate. All of this together means by slowing down, we are in fact speeding up, by becoming more effective and sharper and functioning at our full potential.

It can be difficult to find time for you, especially when you're busy and feel guilty if there are others you're looking after too. But everyone benefits from a better, more refreshed you. Prioritising relaxation and self-care makes us more alive and more effective and allows better decision-making, hence making life easier.

Self-care is something I talk about a lot and also one of my non-negotiables. I learned the hard way back in the corporate world, where the busier I thought I was, the more valued I felt. The more hours I worked, the more status I achieved and the more money I earned, the happier I thought I'd be. It turns out this isn't the formula, and whilst I'm still busy these days, I've mastered the art of balance.

All Blacks skills coach Gilbert Enoka talks about performance waves. We know waves come in sets, and for the All Blacks, the peak of the wave should be game day, when they push hard, compete and perform. But this always needs to be followed by recovery time, a rest day, the calm water we get between the waves. If we try and perform on the peak all the time, it simply isn't sustainable. To get to the peak, we must also experience the calm water and recovery time in between the waves.

I've learned it's critical to my success. This is why I prioritise self-care. It makes me more effective, and it means I can get more done. The bottom line is if we don't make time for self-care, we will need to make time for illness.

I use self-care as the foundation from which I build, and if I feel good and have plenty of energy, everything else seems so much easier, even when the tough times hit. Self-care is a critical part of not only building our resilience but also giving us the mental clarity to create and the energy to succeed.

When we read articles from some of the most successful people in our society, they talk about their morning routines, their self-care, how they centre themselves. I believe this is the key to our success and how we reach our potential, because I've seen the difference it's made for me.

It looks different for everyone. It doesn't have to cost money, take lots of time or be difficult; in fact, the opposite – it makes life easier.

What do you do for your self-care, and is it enough? When do you do it, and how can you find time for more of this in your schedule?

Here are a few ideas:

- Morning meditation
- Walk in nature
- Stretches at home
- Weekly yoga class
- A workout (in the gym or the park)
- Nutrition (planning and preparing meals)
- Adequate sleep
- Gratitude
- Take a few deep breaths
- Put fresh sheets on the bed
- Light your favourite candle

- Play your favourite song
- Call your best friend
- Sit with a cup of tea whilst the house is quiet, before anyone else is up
- Have a bath
- Watch a funny movie
- Learn something new
- Take a swim in the ocean
- Take a day off technology once a month
- Journaling
- Treating yourself – a massage or lunch at your favourite café

It's easy to think going to bed early wastes time that could be spent doing other things, but being fresh and rested saves me time. Not being tired during the day helps me function better, so tasks don't take as long, I focus more, my mind is sharp, problems are solved quicker and the day flows better. This is an investment in time.

Feeling healthy and full of energy helps me cope with what life throws at me, and I'm more inclined to be optimistic, have positive interactions with others (even those who may irritate me) and feel good about myself when I'm not tired and run down. My self-talk is healthier, and I'm less hard on myself – another act of self-care.

I don't mind admitting I'm in bed most nights before 10pm. It means I wake up fresh and ready for the day. I spent years dragging myself out of bed and was desperately attached to the snooze button. As a result, I'd feel sluggish most of the morning and it'd take a few cups of caffeine to lift the brain fog. I find these days my morning routine is so important to starting the day well. My brain functions better, and my mind is more clear and therefore creative.

I get up early, do some stretches and sit for 10 minutes to

meditate, sometimes longer if I've got the time and sometimes not at all if I've not. I believe in the 80:20 rule: if we're doing things 80% of the time, the 20% we miss is inconsequential. I then have breakfast and get ready for the day. I also like to get outside and walk the dog.

Exercise is key for me, as is being out in nature. I make sure this happens in some form most lunchtimes. I also make sure I'm getting to a yoga class at least once a week to offset all the sitting I do. Failing that, I do some stretches at home.

It's the small, simple stuff that makes the difference, the things that don't cost money or take up much extra time, because, let's face it, we need this stuff most because we're so short on time.

Those who know me know I'm a fan of the sauna, particularly in winter. It's a warm, quiet, dark space, and I feel instantly relaxed when I'm in there. It's also where a lot of my thinking happens, so important processing time. It's about having time to ourselves where we can just be and relax – it doesn't necessarily have to be in a sauna.

I'm also a fan of the spa and a massage, but self-care is so much more than this. These are the basics that keep us well, but self-care extends far beyond this. Self-care is also how we allow ourselves to be treated. The people we hang out with, how we allow others to treat us, the voice inside our head and how we let it talk to us. The food we put into our body, the way we feel when we look in the mirror, how busy we allow ourselves to be and if we care enough about ourselves to make time for ourselves.

When we take time for self-care, everyone around us benefits too. If we're compassionate by nature, we can often find we're last on our own list – but then how can we give to others if we're pouring from an empty cup?

So how else can we take care of ourselves and invest in self-care to keep us at our best?

Taking a break from technology once a month for a day or two helps clear my mind and gives me a break from the constant social media messaging and comparison, the not-good-enough spiral it's easy to get caught up in – this is an act of self-care.

Simply sitting in silence for a few minutes before the rest of the house wakes – this is also an act of self-care.

Choosing who my friends are, the people I work with and the work I do each day also contributes to my self-care.

Who we choose to hang around with, the office gossip we engage in and how we let our boss treat us also count as self-care measures that will either add or detract from our wellness and our ability to perform.

Leaving a company that doesn't align to your values, a boss who mistreats you, a partner who doesn't respect you – these are all acts of self-care. As is saying no to demands when you're overscheduled.

Self-care is as much about what we don't do as what we do. Setting good boundaries and saying no as well as delegating. This is critical in ensuring we can perform and something we can struggle with if we're driven to achieve.

Workload, perfectionists and high achievers

I'm a recovering perfectionist, and I've always been driven. Chased my goals and got the greatest satisfaction achieving them. I'm the kind of person who loves crossing things off the to-do list; I'll even add things I've done so I can cross them off and get an achiever high!

Then it's on to the next thing. I'm constantly striving. However, I've noticed as much as I strive, I never seem to arrive. Yes, I may reach my goals, but as fast as I'm approaching them, I'm setting myself new ones, something else to strive for, a new target, more, better.

Now, there's nothing wrong with healthy ambition and a bit

of drive to succeed, but not if we're constantly striving and never arriving; perfectionism can be the undoing of high performance.

Our perfectionist tendencies can also impact on our performance. If we're constantly trying to get everything perfect, we'll likely set ourselves up to fail. We'll also run out of energy, and this will impact our effectiveness. There's a saying: 'Sometimes done is better than perfect.'

Perfectionism can also lead to some poor habits around delegation which further impact our performance. We tend to want more control over what's delivered and think, 'If I don't do it, it won't be done how I want or as good as I'd do it.' So we are reluctant to delegate and take on too much, increasing our overwhelm and impacting our ability to deliver quality work. Ironic, really, when this comes from a place of perfectionism.

We are all on a mission to be the best we can be, to be happy, to have the perfect houses, families, partners and jobs, to complete our to-do lists, to complete our bucket lists, to make our parents proud, to get promoted, earn more money and be successful.

Good enough is no longer enough. It's how we set ourselves up to fail, expect too much and lose touch with reality and where the bar actually is set – often we raise it far higher than it needs to be and sometimes to a point that's not even possible to achieve.

Perfectionism can be our fear of failure manifesting. Sometimes our self-doubt means we're so scared of not making the mark or falling short we go way over what's necessary, work twice as hard, to make sure we don't fail.

Whether we're applying for a job, having our hair done, going to the gym or just doing our day jobs, we want to be the perfect parents, workers, friends and partners.

It's no wonder we're so busy and can never find time for ourselves. We have this superhero complex where we try to juggle multiple roles in life all masterfully. With overflowing to-do lists and excessive demands on our time, there are never enough hours in the day.

The key to beating perfectionism isn't about not doing a good job; it's about resetting the bar to a realistic level and knowing sometimes done is better than perfect. Ensuring the expectations you're setting yourself are realistic and knowing when good enough is exactly that – a job well done.

Whilst perfectionists will always focus on quality and produce good work, they often take longer perfecting that job and spend more time and energy than is required to get it better than excellent. In a time where burnout is becoming so common and we're all short on time and energy, is this really the best use of our resources?

If we're spending extra time perfecting our work, what is it we're not doing with that time, effort and energy? If we stay late to perfect that report at work, we're likely to be out of energy or time to be with the kids that night, for example, or tackle the other things on our to-do list still waiting for our attention.

Perfect, for so long, has been held up as the standard we must aspire to. Anything less is failure – especially in a perfectionist's eyes. Yet we can still over-deliver and exceed expectations without going even further than that to perfect something.

At a conference I attended, I heard Dame Jenny Shipley say, 'The closer you are to perfect, the less people will trust you,' and this really resonates. It changes our quest for perfection into something less desirable and makes a lot of sense to me.

If you're genuine and authentic, I can trust you. If you seem superhuman or not real in some way – too perfect – I'm less likely to connect with you and therefore trust you. It gives us permission to show up as we are and know this is enough. In fact, it's what people are looking for from us if they're going to trust us and see our authenticity.

The trouble with perfect is there's no middle ground. We're

either perfect or it's a failure, and it's often our fear of failure that drives this. We fear failure so much we want to get as far away from it as possible, and of course the other end of the scale is perfect.

We set ourselves up to fail, because perfect doesn't exist, whether it's an airbrushed photo in a magazine we're trying to look like or someone's perfect Facebook life we're comparing to our own, wondering why we're falling short.

Managing the high achiever in you

If you're driven, like me, to achieve your goals, chances are you're a high achiever. It can be dangerous ground to tread. It's closely linked to perfectionism and one of the reasons we're so busy and we can fall victim to our own excessive expectations.

We struggle to relax or utilise downtime because we are so busy but also because we're driven by this need to achieve and be *doing* so much of the time. We can struggle with feelings of guilt, laziness or just being unproductive if we stop for even a moment.

We also don't like to delegate, as we see asking for help as a sign of weakness and also know it'll be quicker if we do it and probably better too. We hate to think of someone else taking longer or not doing it the way we would have. Whilst this means we are high achievers and we get stuff done, we also feel like we're juggling all the balls life throws at us in the air. It's a precarious balancing act and one that at any moment can come crashing down on us. Either we drop one of the balls or we hit a wall completely and burn out – I've done both!

For high achievers, balance can be difficult. How do we ensure we're growing, developing and pushing ourselves but not to our detriment?

High achievers are always busy people, but if we're too busy, we burn out. We're also tired a lot of the time from all our achieving, and this means we're probably not performing at our best.

As high achievers, failure is our worst nightmare. It's proof our self-doubting, negative self-talk is right, and it's at odds with our need to achieve everything we attempt, so we try to avoid it completely.

The danger is if we're too afraid to fail, we might not even try. It can lead to us leaning out, not in, and can mean we opt for the easy route and stick to what we know so we're guaranteed success and achievement.

If we do this, we stop growing, we don't get out of our comfort zone and we miss out on a huge part of our development and potential.

Let's face it: if any of the above is true, chances are we're about to come unstuck anyway, so we need another way!

Here are some top tips for high achievers:

- Give yourself permission to make mistakes
- Know you don't have to be a superhero to be enough and to be worthy
- Stop comparing yourself to others
- Remember sometimes done is better than perfect
- Don't beat yourself up when you fall short – we're all human
- Put yourself first for a change
- Remember you can't pour from an empty cup
- Don't expect brilliance 100% of the time just because you're capable of it
- Know your performance will suffer if you're tired and stressed out
- Make time for self-care – balance the busyness and build resilience
- Leverage your strengths rather than trying to be good at everything
- Ask for help when you need it, and delegate tasks

- Remember the to-do list will never be complete
- Remind yourself you're doing the best you can with what you've got, and that is enough

Top tips to manage workload

NZ Stats found a direct correlation between stress and dissatisfaction at work. Of those who experienced stress in the last year, 19% were dissatisfied with their job, compared to 1.5% of those who didn't experience stress.

Stress and overwhelm are common complaints in our works days. Long hours and overflowing to-do lists will impact our ability to perform, as will the stress we feel.

The impacts on our health and happiness are also well documented these days. Yet still so many of us experience stress most days and think this is normal, an expected part of our job or modern life, and it's costing us.

There are ways to deal with stress and workloads, and all of them revolve around the choices we make and how we choose to show up. We are accountable for the stress we feel. That might sound harsh, and you may be thinking, 'You don't work for my boss.' Sure, a boss and a business can cause stress; if we work in a toxic culture or are being bullied, we're likely to feel stress. We choose what we do about that, though.

Let's focus on workload. Whilst our businesses may set our hours and job descriptions, most of the time we can choose how we deliver that work. There might be days we're under the pump because of staff shortages, breakdowns, and systems and processes that make life harder, not easier, but that's something we can navigate and lobby to change.

Our to-do list and hours worked tend to be something we control, in so much as we choose what we do when and what needs to be done first. There will be times there's an emergency or the boss needs something yesterday, but these are generally exceptions, not rules.

When working from home during Covid-19, many people reported an increase in hours. Now, this wasn't the boss telling us we had to be in at a certain time or meetings being booked at 7am. This was our choice. We got up at the same time, and instead of the commute, we went straight to our laptop. We forgot to stop for lunch or take a break because we were at home so didn't have to go anywhere, and then we worked past 5pm because we didn't need to go and fetch the kids, because they were already at home. We chose to extend our work schedules. Some of us were busy because of Covid-19 contingency planning, but we're never too busy to take a proper break.

We've already talked about the impacts of this and the difference between busy and productive. This attachment to busy also breeds the feeling everything is urgent and must be done now, whether it's the to-do list I just wrote or the emails that came in over the last hour. Not everything on the to-do list is an emergency; the to-do list will also never be clear. Those emails don't need responding to now (some will, so do those, but leave the rest until tomorrow or pass them to someone else to deal with).

I love the rocks and sand analogy, which allows us to focus on our priorities in the allotted time we have available. If I have a jar (my hours in the day) and some rocks (important things I have to do) and sand (less important things I have to do), I'll find if I try and put the sand in first there's no room left for the big rocks and I miss getting the important stuff done; I run out of room. However, if I put the rocks in first, I'll find the sand fits easily between the cracks and there's enough room in the jar (or hours in the day).

We can also section our to-do list off based on what's important for today and what's left over (that is, things we'll schedule for another day or delegate to someone else).

I'll often have a Post-it over my weekly to-do list with my focus items for today, the most important things from that to-do list

I need to do today.

One of the main ways to manage our workload, though, is to manage our mindset. If we believe our workload is overwhelming and we're too busy, that's exactly how we'll feel. Mindset is critical and what we'll look at next.

> **'This has made me a "done is better than perfect" person'**
>
> *Christine Langdon left the corporate world and a career in communications to found social enterprise The Good Registry.*
>
> I was lucky at school I knew what I wanted to do. I wanted to be a journalist and write creatively, because I was good at it, I was curious and I asked lots of questions. I loved this as a career but got to the point where I hit a ceiling. I didn't want to be in the newsroom forever and did not want to move into management either. Just because you're good at something doesn't mean you'll enjoy being promoted and paid more to manage people. I wanted to be chasing the news, not sitting at a desk managing performance.
>
> I had an opportunity to take redundancy, and I didn't know what else I would do but opened myself up to the possibilities. One of the themes for me through these changes is when your cup is full and you've got a lot on, there's no room for new stuff to come in; leave room for opportunities, and sometimes that means leaving secure employment without a plan.
>
> A second career I loved grew through communications roles I took. I was making good money and learning a lot, but I got to that point at the end of each week of hollowness. I felt like I'd had a good week with great people, but something felt like it was missing. I started to fill that with volunteering. I taught yoga in prison and noticed this really filled my cup –

the contribution. That insight led me to leave my corporate career and look for ways to get more of that joy I found in contributing.

I didn't have a plan; I just wanted to take some time to do the things I didn't have time for when I was busy working. I wanted to make a difference and also earn a living, and throw myself into something I believed in.

The Good Registry was a chance to create something with my skills and also make a difference in the world. Where are we currently wasting money and resources, and how could we put it towards good instead? The idea came whilst decluttering the house and finding unused gifts in cupboards and drawers, and then having a birthday and receiving more stuff I didn't need. It made me sad that loved ones had chosen these gifts – the environmental impact of the production, and all for something I didn't really need or use. Having support from those around me and learning the things I didn't know really helped. It was a quick turnaround, though, because we had decided to launch in time for Christmas. I didn't want to wait a whole year, and this was the best time to launch a gift-giving business. I have always wanted to get things right, but this has made me become a much more 'done is better than perfect' person.

I've always enjoyed my work, but now I get to see the positive difference my work makes, and it's worth the challenges and the hard stuff I have to learn how to do.

My advice is start doing the things you love, outside of work, at least. Instead of watching TV or filling time, find something that feeds your soul and do that outside of work. For me, this was teaching yoga and volunteering.

Many people said, 'I'd love to do what you're doing but can't.' Think about how you can. For many people, it's the salary we think we need, and I tread carefully here, because we're all different, but I think we generally think we need more than we do. A lot of our expenses could be trimmed back. My cost of living has gone down so much, and I've realised there are so many ways to enjoy life that don't come at the expense I used to think was essential.

Mindset

We've looked at the role of balance and how we build resilience; this enables us to perform and gives us the energy to manage our workloads. Before we look at the power of habits and how to maintain habits for good performance, we first must understand the role of mindset and how to master the mind.

The mind is so powerful and plays such a critical role in how we show up and how happy we are, and obviously this applies to both work and life. You know the difference between the glass-half-empty people you know and the glass-half-full – it's the lens they view life through, and that starts in the mind.

Mastering our mind is crucial not just for balance and calm but for effectiveness and self-efficacy too.

Our brains are so busy. One of the reasons we feel so overwhelmed is the amount of information rushing through our mind at any given time. This is all the things we have to do along with all the worries we have, what others think, regrets of the past and plans for the future.

When we think about how busy life has become, how much there is on our schedule and the expectations we place on ourselves, both at home and at work, it can be overwhelming. Sometimes the mind feels full of fog, with a million and one things buzzing around in there, without the space to think about any of them clearly.

Language is so important, because if we tell ourselves something often enough, our mind will think it's true. It's why if we tell ourselves we're not pretty, we'll not like what we see in the mirror. Similarly, if we tell ourselves and everyone around us we're so stressed and busy all the time, our mind will become overwhelmed.

When I learned to meditate, I became more self-aware; I began to get in touch with who I was and what I wanted, but I also became more aware of what was going on in my mind. This gave me an ability to choose to respond rather than react to emotions that came up. It also helped slow the tide of thoughts and noise to develop a calmer, clearer, more peaceful mind.

Before we can cultivate a positive mindset, we must make room in the mind and calm its busyness. If our minds are busy and full, we struggle to think straight. Becoming more calm in our mind is the quickest way to overcome overwhelm and manage anxiety. It's something I spent a decade of my life studying across the world, and I have had a daily practice ever since.

I've combined what I've learned from various traditions and cultures and made it relatable to our modern Western lives. I've spent time in Plum Village, Thich Nhat Hanh's retreat centre in France; living with Buddhist monks in northern Thailand, teaching them English whilst immersing myself in their culture; and in Bhutan, the kingdom famous for measuring gross national happiness in place of GDP.

I trained to be a yoga teacher in 2014 in Australia, but rather than the physical asana practice, mindfulness, meditation and the mental side of yoga became my passion and where I've chosen to focus since. It is something I've delivered to corporate offices, medical practices, lawyers, community groups and more.

Having studied with Buddhist monks and nuns across a decade and lived in ashrams and retreat centres across the world, I understand not only the impact our mindset has on our life but also how we can learn to train it.

This has been the turning point for me and the one thing out of everything I've learned in life I will continue to prioritise. It makes such a difference and is so important to how I function, how I react to tough times and how I bounce back and manage my busyness. That's why it's such a passion and one I love to share.

We are what we think. Our thoughts make our worlds. Everything we do and feel starts in the mind and is influenced by how we think. Therefore, it makes sense we should look after our minds, but how often do we spend time taking care of them? Imagine if we spent as much time and effort looking after our minds as we do our bodies. All the products, beauty treatments, diets, gyms and so on. What do we do for the mind? The statistics would suggest the answer is not enough. In fact, the statistics may imply we are paying a high price for living like we do.

In 2019 Statistics New Zealand told us that one in four adults experiences poor mental health, according to the World Health Organization's five-point scale. The WHO itself estimates approximately 450 million people worldwide have a mental health problem and by 2030 depression will be the second-highest cause of disease burden in middle-income countries.

The mind is an amazing place and also something we cannot escape from, regardless of how much money we have, how far we travel or how popular we are. Our mind will always be there, and so will the thoughts we put in it, which is why it's important to ensure those thoughts are positive, helpful ones.

We take our thoughts with us everywhere we go. If we're having unhappy thoughts, it doesn't matter if we're at a five-star tropical resort in the sun; we'll still feel unhappy. Or, as monk Matthieu Ricard puts it, 'If you're having suicidal thoughts and someone gives you a luxury penthouse apartment, all you're going to do is look for a window from which to jump.'

Much of the time, we don't even know what's happening in our minds – we're too busy to notice the chatter. We're not sure what it's up to and whether this is helpful for us or not.

Imagine if a megaphone broadcast all your thoughts for the duration of today – what impacts that would have. You may not have a job, many friends or a relationship by the end of the day!

Yet this stuff is going on in there all the time. We can have a barrage of negative self-talk happening in our minds and not even be aware of it.

Our minds are wired to think more negatively, so it makes it an uphill battle to try and train the mind to think more positively, yet it is key to helping build our resilience and weather life's storms. Many major sports teams have tapped into the power of positive thinking, and many businesses now leverage the power of positive psychology.

After all, it all begins in the mind. What we think becomes how we feel, and that in turn becomes how we act and the results and outcomes we experience. This is why it's so critical our minds are positive, not negative, places.

In our busy lives, we are often on autopilot. We get lost in the doing at the expense of being. Have you ever arrived at work and not remembered the commute? It's when we are focusing on other things and our minds have wandered that we are not paying attention and life passes us by.

A 2010 *Harvard Business Review* article on multitasking found it is in fact a myth. When our brains are seemingly multitasking, what they're actually doing is switching from one thing to another in very quick succession, often microseconds.

So we must ask ourselves what quality we are giving these simultaneous thoughts when we're multitasking. If we can't actually do many things at once, are we doing them justice by trying to?

In a world where multitasking is seen as a necessary skill, being mindful is the opposite. It is slowing down to focus on one thing at a time, one moment at a time, full concentration, unwavering attention on one thing.

Thoughts will still come, and this is natural. We are not trying to stop or supress our thoughts, but we become witnesses or observers to what comes up. Without judging what we find, we notice the thought and return to being mindful without attaching to what that thought means or being carried away by analysing it.

We can start by breathing mindfully and being aware of the breath, whether we are sitting meditating, in the car driving to work or queuing at the supermarket. Eating mindfully is another helpful practice – not only does it help slow us down and focus on our food, but it's better for our digestion than rushing through our meals.

Mindful walking is a lovely way to spend a summer's evening – there is no destination in mind, it is slow and deliberate, we're not rushing from point A to point B, nor are we lost in thought about what went on at work that day. We are mindfully absorbed in the joy of walking, feeling the ground beneath our feet, listening to the birds in the trees, feeling the breeze in our face and watching the sun sinking in the sky.

Science is catching up with what ancient wisdom has always known, with many studies proving regular meditation physically changes the brain, including benefits like making us calm, compassionate and more aware and also aiding sleep, memory, emotional regulation and problem-solving, thus improving our mood.

When I sit still for just 10 minutes a day (sometimes five if I'm short on time), I recentre; I have an opportunity to notice what's going on inside me, seeing what comes up but most importantly slowing down, resting my brain and training it to focus.

This focus remains long after I've stopped meditating. My mind becomes clear and sharp all the time. It's like our muscles becoming strong when we've been to the gym regularly for a while. We're strong not just whilst we're at the gym but all the time.

I focus on my breathing during my meditations; many times I get distracted by thoughts, but that's normal. It's the constant act of coming back to the breath that trains the brain to focus. When I'm focused on the breath, my mind stills and I can't simultaneously be focused on thoughts, negativity or worries, so I become calm.

It's like being able to access a clear blue sky on a cloudy day. Regardless of how many clouds are in the sky today, if you got in a plane and went above the clouds, the sun would be shining and the sky blue. This is like the mind: we always have access to sunshine and clear blue if we allow the clouds to subside.

This is different from trying to constrain thoughts; it's more about letting them pass through, like clouds in the sky. I love the analogy of muddy water to explain this. If I scoop muddy water out of a puddle into a glass, it's generally murky and mixed up, much like a busy mind. If I leave the glass still on the table, the sediment settles and sinks to the bottom, leaving clear water on top. This is like the mind when meditating: the thoughts and sediment subside, and clarity and stillness appear.

For me, it's about having a toolkit to tap into when my brain becomes busy. Taking some deep breaths each morning before I begin my day or recentring after a tough day. When we still our mind, the important stuff floats to the top, rather than the noise of all the busyness we're constantly faced with.

My gratitude practice also helps me train the brain to be a more positive place to be and helps me notice more of the good that exists.

Technology and the mind

Our relationship with technology also impacts our mindset, busyness and mood.

Whilst technology has revolutionised the way we live and work, we are now also starting to see the mental health impacts of our constant connection to devices and how it overloads our already busy brain.

Now, I don't think technology is bad; it's amazing, and it has some real life-improving uses, not just for keeping in touch with friends and family overseas, disaster management, health apps and more. It's critical for my business – but it's also critical for my health that I monitor the amount of time I spend using it.

It's not so much technology that's the problem but rather our relationship with it. Like everything, in moderation it can be good, but that's the problem – we've never been very good at moderation as humans in the developed world!

We used to have many pauses during our normal day. Time to rest and reset the mind. Times we're waiting for the kettle to boil, the bus to arrive for work, the lift to the next floor, the supermarket queue. Now, during those times our minds used to be idling, resting and checking in with ourselves, we're absorbing many more thoughts, emotions and information.

Most people report their minds feeling busy, full and overloaded; some would even go as far as to say crazy, messy, stressed, anxious, depressed. Scrolling through our devices or spending four hours a day on social media is going to make this worse, not better.

If it's the first thing we reach for when we wake up, we might have looked at the weather forecast, checked the news headlines, replied to friends' messages, watched a few cat videos, scrolled through some Instagram photos and liked a few Facebook posts all before we've even got out of bed.

Imagine how much information we've just placed in our busy brain before we even get up and think about the day ahead and the things we have to do – and we wonder why we can't think straight. A similar routine might play out at the end of the day, when we go to bed, and we wonder why we struggle to sleep.

According to recent findings, an average person checks their phone about 63 times a day.

Eighty-seven per cent of us do it one hour before going to bed, while 69% of us check smartphones within the first five minutes of waking up.

When we're lost in our device, we're less present and, as a result, much more distracted, to the point where some of us can't cross the road safely anymore, such is our attachment to our device and our connection to the virtual world.

We live in a digitally distracted world. Technology is key to how we live our life, yet it impacts our mental health and our ability to perform. So how do we balance this?

I've removed my notifications – when I check my emails or Facebook, it's a once-a-day occurrence and something I've done intentionally. I've not been tricked into logging on for the tenth time that day because of a red notification badge. It also means if I pick my phone up to check the weather, I don't get distracted by a notification and find myself 30 minutes later watching videos of baby goats.

Allow your device to monitor your usage, and set goals or downtime periods so your device is actually helping you develop healthier habits around its usage. Use the data it collects to be aware of how much you're using your device and specific apps on it and have an idea of what's reasonable for you.

Set times for checking messages and media – maybe in the morning and then after lunch – and resolve not to pick up your device between times. Don't keep it close to hand. Have device-free zones in the house. The dinner table and the bedroom are great starting points. Or a no-devices-after-9pm rule might work for your family.

Definitely don't take it to bed. It's hard when so many of us use it as an alarm, but if it's in the bedroom, it's likely to be the first thing we look at and the last thing we do before sleep. We know the LED screen interrupts our melatonin production, therefore interfering with sleep. If we wake up in the middle of the night, the worst thing we can do is start scrolling if we want to get back to sleep.

Going to sleep is supposed to be a time we slow down the brain, begin to unplug and switch off. If we're scrolling through the news, checking our emails, putting filters on our selfies and comparing our life to what other people are posting, imagine what our brain is doing when we get into bed.

No wonder we feel overwhelmed, busy-brained, confused, anxious and overloaded. I believe our relationship with our devices is contributing massively in this space.

This is even more important where our work device is concerned, because all that becomes much more stressful and overwhelming if it's work emails and staff conversations on Slack.

Yes, we all have busy lives and challenges in the real world, but that's even more reason to create the space in our brain to process and deal with this rather than busying it further with our device habits and information overload.

It's why I also try and make a device-free day once a month. I switch off my phone and put it in a drawer, even if it's just from 8am to 8pm on a Sunday. It's amazing what a break our mind gets when we do this and how much more time we find in our day to do other things.

Fixed and growth mindset

Our mind is a powerful thing. The stories we tell ourselves and the things we believe can either prevent change from happening or allow new skills to develop. This is something often referred to as the fixed or growth mindset, which Stanford psychologist Carol Dweck examined in her best-selling book *Mindset*.

Over 30 years ago, Dweck and her colleagues became interested in students' attitudes about failure. They noticed some students rebounded, while others seemed devastated by even the smallest setbacks. After studying the behaviour of thousands of students, Dweck coined the terms fixed mindset and growth mindset.

Dweck says, 'In a fixed mindset students believe their basic abilities, their intelligence, their talents, are just fixed traits. They have a certain amount and that's that, and then their goal becomes to look smart all the time and never look dumb. In a growth mindset students understand their talents and abilities can be developed through effort, good teaching and persistence. They believe everyone can get smarter if they work at it.'

A growth mindset thrives on challenge, sees failure as an opportunity to grow and believes we can learn anything we want. Challenges are opportunities to help us grow, and we'll enjoy trying new things, seeking feedback and being inspired by the success of others.

In a fixed mindset, we believe failure is a limit of our abilities and cannot be changed. We're either good at it or we're not. We believe talent alone leads to success, and so effort is not required. We don't like to be challenged in this mindset, preferring to play it safe and do what we know, so we don't risk failing. We tend to take feedback and criticism personally, and when we get frustrated, we give up.

For example, my fixed mindset tells me I'm not good at maths, so I can't do budgets and accounts; it's why I hate the end-of-year tax returns. With a growth mindset, this becomes, 'I need to learn how to budget and do my accounts, because maths is not my strength. I'd like to develop this skill and tackle the challenge of my end-of-year accounts.'

Dweck talks about the example of a school in Chicago that, rather than give a failing grade, gives the grade 'not yet', encouraging a growth mindset in the kids. They're on a learning curve and on a path into the future where they can learn and improve, so the next time they take that test, it might be a pass. Dweck advises we praise our kids wisely. Praising our kids for talent or intelligence has failed, with a result of kids who get praised for everything fearing failure or not 'winning' and therefore playing it safe and not risking failing. She tells us we should praise for effort, perseverance, improvement or progress, to encourage kids to try and take risks, to fail and learn – this also helps raise resilient kids, Dweck says.

At the heart of what makes the growth mindset so good for our development, Dweck found, is it creates a passion for learning, rather than a hunger for approval. Not only are people with this mindset not discouraged by failure, but they don't actually see themselves as failing in those situations – they see themselves as learning!

Neuroplasticity means the brain can change and that a growth mindset can be taught. It starts with being aware of our thinking patterns. Embrace challenges as an opportunity to grow, and focus on the process rather than the end result. If we give ourselves permission to fail, we'll see it's how we learn and therefore a positive when we're in a growth mindset.

'As you think, so you become'

Anamika is a civil engineer.

I work in water and wastewater infrastructure design, helping councils assess their infrastructure capabilities to cater for future growth and demand. I wanted to do something that would make an impact, and I knew water would be our new gold. In future years, it'll be harder to get clean, fresh water to our taps, and that's something we currently take for granted.

As a child I always hated seeing people waste water, and I wanted to make a change. I'm passionate about looking at alternative water options for the future. I'm a passionate learner too, and that's part of my growth, continuous learning and trying new things; it keeps my mind busy.

The job works with my skill set of problem-solving. When I'm given a task, I have to come up with a solution and it has to be quick. In meetings I'm constantly absorbing information like a sponge and figuring out solutions for the client; it involves a lot of listening. I like the critical thinking part of the job, although it can get stressful at times. I enjoy talking to more experienced people and experts so I can learn more about things.

I didn't know what university I wanted to go to or what to study like my classmates did. I wanted to keep my options open, so I took science and maths. I really enjoyed my study, and this, along with my passion for water and the fact the course was available where I lived, pushed me towards this job. It was the best choice I've made.

When I started studying, I was the only girl in my class. It didn't put me off, though; I was unique and diverse, and I was outperforming the boys in the class, which gave me more confidence, so I thought, 'I can do exactly what they do.' Now there are more female engineers in my current workplace.

My advice to others is to take the time to think about what you want to do; you will find it. Don't pick something just because you feel you have to. Understand what your interests are and talk to people who know more about those areas so they can give you an insight into different career paths.

It always gives me great peace of mind to wake up in the morning and realise that if things don't work out, there is always another way; I get to make the choice. A Sanskrit phrase from Rigveda I like quoting to myself – 'yad bhāvam tad bhavati', which means 'as you think, so you become'.

The power of habits

To conclude this section on high performance, we really need to talk about the power of habits. After all, high performance comes from setting good habits. This is certainly what I've seen work for me and the recurring themes I've observed across high-performing individuals I've worked with.

How they look after themselves and build resilience is key and impacts their mindset, which we know is a crucial difference between success and failure. The key to getting those bits right, though, often is within the habits they form. This is how we hit peak performance – forming good habits and breaking bad ones.

It sounds simple, but it's not. Otherwise, we'd all go to the gym, eat salad and wake up at 6am every day. Even when we know the negative impacts of a habit, it can be hard to break. Think of smoking as an example; we know it kills us, but sometimes that's still not enough to stop us.

A habit is a repeated behaviour that becomes automatic. The trouble is we tend to find it easier to keep the bad habits and harder to form good ones – it's more effort and often less immediate reward.

Our bad habits work against us by being easy to perform and giving instant hits of reward – a wine on a Friday night, for example. Good habits tend to have delayed reward and are harder to perform as a result. Eating well won't give us an immediate sugar hit, and the health benefits or weight loss might not come until weeks down the track.

How can we build positive habits and break bad ones? The best advice I've heard on this topic comes from James Clear and his book *Atomic Habits*. Clear believes that both success and failure are preceded by habits, and we can be the creator of our habits, not the victim. What's on our desk or how we set up our home can influence our behaviours and habits – often, he says, our environment is the architect of our habits.

What I like about focusing on our habits is that it puts us in control; it's something we can influence. Whilst we tend to think success is down to talent and some people are just high performers because of talent, there's much more to it. Talent gets us so far, but great habits make the difference. It makes sense when we look at those who are talented; at some point, they're going to reach a peak where everyone else around them is just as talented, so how do they stand out? Good habits, continuous improvement and a drive for performance. This is true when we hear the stories of top athletes. They may have talent to start with, but so do others who've not made it in their field. The difference most of them talk about is the hard work and effort they put in.

It's about forming good habits and repeating them consistently, whether that's your gym routine and training or organising your diary, doing your filing, taking a lunch break and checking in on your team.

Let's look at breaking bad habits first, though. Reducing exposure and temptation is key. If you want to save money, unsubscribe from those marketing emails that tempt you with specials. Want to stop eating chocolate at night whilst watching TV? Don't buy it or have it in the house. If we have to get in the car and go to the shops for it, we're less likely to do it – making the bad habit harder helps break it.

Is your environment conducive to forming good habits or bad ones? Which are easier for you, and how can you make the bad ones harder to do and the good ones easier? I don't have biscuits in the house usually; it's an easy way to break my bad habit of demolishing a whole packet at once. Similarly, having my gym kit ready to go in the morning means I'm more likely to go to the gym – I've made it easier.

It's the law of least effort, according to Clear. If we make bad habits harder and good habits easier, we'll see a shift. We also have to want to do the habit (enjoy it) and have an environment that's conducive and a plan to make it happen.

The law of least effort is why it's easy to binge-watch Netflix. The environment is created in a way that means it's easier to let it keep autoplaying the next episode than to pick up the device and press stop. It's why we plan on watching one episode and instead watch the whole season and stay up three hours later than planned!

It's why I go on retreat to write books. It removes distractions, and I find less excuses not to write when I'm away in the countryside, in a cottage, by myself. I don't have TV or take books; it's just me and my writing. I also have to make it rewarding, though, so I take my favourite snacks and give myself a target. Each day, when I hit the word count, I reward myself with a cup of tea and some chocolate biscuits. There's that instant gratification, a reward that comes much sooner than seeing the book on the shelf.

So how can we form good habits and make them easier to adopt? Simply by doing that: making them easy and linking them to a reward, so we enjoy doing them.

I love the sauna, but the gym takes a bit more motivation. They are based in the same building, so leaving my gym kit ready to go in the car makes it easy for me to go (or at least gives me less excuses not to), and then I reward myself afterwards with a sauna. I know I only get the sauna if I go to the gym, and once I'm in the building for one, the other becomes much easier to stick to.

There is another great hack from James Clear when it comes to forming good habits: habit stacking. Adding a new habit you want to form on to an existing habit, so you're more likely to do it.

For example, I mean to take my supplements, but I often forget. Leaving them by the kettle helps remind me and make this habit easy, because I've stacked it with another habit I know I'll do every morning – my cup of tea.

Similarly, my meditation habit is something I do each morning for 10 minutes at the same time my partner is walking the dog. It means the house is quiet, and it's part of my routine before my shower.

When we think of habits, it can become a drain – I must do this. Reframing this into 'the kind of person I want to become' gives it more meaning and also motivates us.

I want to be a calm, clear-headed, happy individual; that's why I meditate each morning. That's different from thinking of it as another thing on my to-do list I've got to get around to doing today. It connects with my why and the benefit I'm getting from this. It links my results to my beliefs. There's also the added reward hit on my meditation app, which gives me a gold star each time I don't miss a day, because, let's face it, the reward of a calm, clear mind takes much more than one session to realise.

So, what habits do you want to form, and what's your plan of action? Having the goal is one thing, but James Clear will tell you that the habit is the system behind making that goal a reality.

Our fitness or weight-loss goals only happen because of healthy habits. Our revenue goals are realised because of our sales strategy, so it's less about what we're aiming for and more about what we're going to do to get there – then the result takes care of itself.

This enables us to have a plan and develop good habits. I really like the analogy Clear uses of running a race; we tend to focus on the finish line and how we ready ourselves for the result we want to see. Clear looks at it more like being ready for the start line. If we're ready at the start line, the finish (goal) will take care of itself and eventuate by virtue of our preparation and plan (habits).

If we get to the gym after work and we've already put our gym kit in the car the night before, we've done the hard work; the chances are we'll work out now rather than turning around and going home.

It's also worth noting for this not to seem unachievable and overwhelming, Clear advises focusing on one habit at a time and making a 1% improvement. This is achievable and still impactful as it compounds. If all you can do is meditate for a minute, that's okay; you're still forming the habit. Similarly, if you roll the yoga mat out and only do one pose, you've made the effort and formed the habit; it'll grow from there. This 1% improvement philosophy helps us take this on in a manageable way. Small improvements lead to big changes; they add up and help our performance.

As for Clear himself, he's a constant student and loves learning, another indicator of high performers. Learn from others. Who do you admire and why? What is it that they do?

'Just make a start'

Anna runs video production company Flying Saucer with partner Hamish, a sea kayak guide she met in Abel Tasman National Park in 2005.

With Hamish's marketing and tourism knowledge and my background in production in the film industry, we embarked on a business idea together that fit with our desired lifestyle. We were both aligned on living our best lives and being in the moment, and we wanted to work together doing that. We were into physical activity, the outdoors and going on adventures, rather than being in a corporate job, earning money to retire early.

So we bought a camera and a laptop and started driving Hamish's old car around the country, filming promotional videos for local tourism businesses. We'd often just call people up and ask to camp in their backyard in exchange for the shoot. We met so many interesting people and had some awesome adventures. People are incredibly generous. If they can see you're really into what you're doing and enjoy it, they'll open up and share their hospitality with you. Diving into someone's zone with a camera can be quite intrusive, so it's a privilege when people open their lives to you in this way.

Money was tight in the early days. I don't ever remember feeling stressed, though, because we were having such a great time. We put ourselves into some crazy situations where we had no idea what we were doing but learned so much.

Our first paid gig took us up in a helicopter to the back country of the Remarkables in Queenstown, to shoot a promo video for a snowboard clothing label. We turned up with borrowed equipment we were learning to use the night before, and I hadn't been on the snow for a decade. We had a great time; we were all into adventure and became friends. Fourteen years on, we've learned a lot and Flying Saucer has grown, but we're still built on those same principles of being curious about people and the environment. We can be driving for four hours on a 4WD track way out into the countryside to film beekeepers, for example, then the farmer turns up with a BBQ on the back of his truck and creates a beautiful lunch in the middle of nowhere.

The most satisfying part is telling inspiring stories about things people perhaps wouldn't have known about before. We want the business to sustain a diverse range of people, so we do some outreach with the local universities, fostering new talent via our graduates, incorporating their freshness and ideas into what we do and helping them gain experience in the industry.

My advice to others considering this kind of move would be go for it, if your risk is low. We just went for it, but that was before children! Dive in, start small and pick the low-hanging fruit and expand from there. Always network, go to the events, meet with groups and be interested in what others are doing. Have your business plan, but also be open to opportunities. You can spend your whole life researching what you should and shouldn't do on the internet; just get in there. Just make a start.

Conclusion

Once we've found a job that aligns to our values and strengths, it's so much easier to perform well. We get satisfaction and achievement from the work we do, and we can see the difference it makes, bringing purpose and passion into our life.

We spend so much of our time at work; of course it makes sense we enjoy it, but so many of us don't, and I hope this book can change that in some way. I remember what it was like to be stuck in a job that suffocated my soul, feeling like there must be more to it than this but always pulled back by the money, other people's expectations or the fear of doing anything different.

I also now know what it's like to be on the other side of that and do a job that doesn't feel like work at all. I never thought I'd be disappointed when a public holiday rolled around, but these days I love what I do and want to do it often. This is what passion looks like, and once we know where our passions lie and what brings purpose to why we do what we do, things become so much clearer. It doesn't mean we have to quit our job, run our own business or work for a charity, saving lives. We're all different, and passion and purpose comes in many forms.

I wanted to include stories from others to demonstrate where this has been done and what the impacts have been and to help us understand it isn't necessary to be stuck in a job we don't enjoy just for the money.

Whilst the path is not always easy, it is possible to do work we love and get paid for it. I hope I've presented a compelling argument against the societal model of career success that revolves around status, titles and salary. To allow us to tap into our intrinsic motivation of passion, purpose and happiness.

I hope this book has helped you reflect on your career and discover your why. To know your values and strengths and check if that aligns to what you're doing now. If you've decided to make the move, congratulations and well done on being brave for making that step.

No job is ever wasted, and there'll be experiences that have taught you valuable lessons along this journey, as well as skills you've picked up that'll transfer with you. I feel grateful for the years I spent in human resources, and the skills and experience I gained I often use in this work, especially for topics such as this one.

Having known what it's like, been on the journey myself as well as witnessing it in so many others, it's my pleasure to share this in a way I hope helps others. This isn't about us all quitting our jobs but about reassessing our career plans and what the next move looks like in a bid to wake up happy that it's Monday again – whilst still paying the bills and learning.

The practical guidance I've included from my varied HR career I hope gives you an insight into what goes on on the other side of the table during recruitment processes and an inside edge that'll help your own preparation, for those of you looking to make a move.

For those experiencing difficulties with your boss or a toxic work culture, a move away might be even more necessary for you, and I'd encourage you to seek some help and support through your employee assistance programme or similar. Before we consider any of what I've written here, we need to ensure the basics around safety in our workplace – the impacts of not doing so can be detrimental to our confidence and health.

No matter what our jobs, there will always be challenges, which is why I felt it important to talk about resilience, work–life balance and mindset. These are key ingredients regardless of how much we love Mondays. In fact, if we love Mondays, we might find we're even more inclined to work longer and prioritise our work over other areas of our life. First we have to know ourselves, believe in ourselves and, of course, look after ourselves to be at our best.

You're now a step closer to finding joy in your work, loving your Mondays and all of the benefits that brings for our health, relationships and happiness, not to mention the gift we give to the world.

I believe if we all worked to our strengths and did work we loved, not only would we be healthier and happier but our businesses would be so much more productive and innovative too. Good things happen when we're connected to our purpose, leveraging our strengths and aligned to our values, and this is my wish for you.

I hope one day more of us are able to jump out of bed each Monday morning knowing we make a difference, perform at our best and continue to grow in a career we love.

Resources

JESS RUNS ONE-TO-ONE coaching sessions, working alongside you to put these words into practice and set a plan in place for your future career.

She also runs workshops on mindset, belief, resilience and leadership development, as well as specific women in leadership programmes.

She is available as a keynote speaker for your event. See www. jessstuart.co.nz for more details.

Acknowledgements

I'D LIKE TO thank all those who support me in making this happen and enable me to do a job I love. Those who help me put my words into print, those who have supported me personally on this journey and those who continue to turn up to my events and offer feedback and messages of thanks.

A special thanks to all those who took the time to talk to me about their jobs, what they love and the journey to getting there, including the industry experts who allowed me to pick their brains. This book is so much better because of your input.

I also want to acknowledge those who are not enjoying their job right now and hope this will help you change that.

Thanks to my editor, my PR team, my designers and my printers. To my loving parents, family, friends and wife, I'm eternally grateful and love you all.

To all those who listen to me speak and read my words, I feel privileged to have been part of your journey.

Arohanui.

About the author

Jess Stuart is an author, coach and international speaker who empowers people to be their best.

A highly acclaimed event speaker, Jess has been featured on Three's *The Café*, the BBC, Radio New Zealand, Stuff, Tiny Buddha and Elephant Journal and in the *Dominion Post* and *NZBusiness* magazine.

She helps busy high achievers find more time for themselves, reprioritise what matters, build resilience, beat the overwhelm, keep calm in the chaos, realise their potential and believe they can.

With a background in senior HR roles and a decade in the corporate world, Jess believes tapping into your potential doesn't mean doing more or having to be different. It's uncovering what's already there and being enough as you are.

Born in Leicestershire, England, Jess now lives in Wellington, New Zealand, with her wife and their dog. Outside of work, she'll be found at the beach, on road trips close to nature and the ocean or sitting quietly in the sun. A foodie, she loves dining out, cooking at home and just eating delicious food in general. A daily yoga and meditation practice keeps her grounded and gives her the energy for the work she loves. Regular trips back to spend time with family in the UK are a must for Jess, who considers herself a Kiwi now.